The
Healing Spirit
of
Haiku

THE
Healing Spirit
OF
Haiku

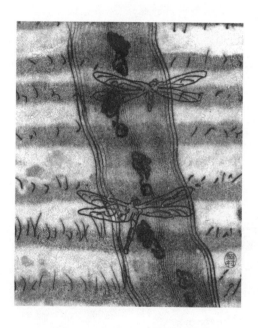

David Rosen & Joel Weishaus

with illustrations by ARTHUR OKAMURA

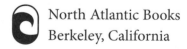
North Atlantic Books
Berkeley, California

Published by:
North Atlantic Books
Berkeley, California 94712

Cover design by Paula Morrison

Book design by Jan Camp

Cover monoprint by Arthur Okamura

Printed in the United States of America

Distributed to the book trade by Publishers Group West

The Healing Spirit of Haiku is sponsored by the Society for the Study of Native Arts and Sciences, a nonprofit educational corporation whose goals are to develop an educational and crosscultural perspective linking various scientific, social, and artistic fields; to nurture a holistic view of arts, sciences, humanities, and healing; and to publish and distribute literature on the relationship of mind, body, and nature.

North Atlantic Books' publications are available through most bookstores. For further information, call 800-337-2665 or visit our website at www.northatlanticbooks.com.

Substantial discounts on bulk quantities are available to corporations, professional associations, and other organizations. For details and discount information, contact our special sales department.

Library of Congress Cataloging-in-Publication Data

Rosen, David H., 1945–
The healing spirit of haiku / by David Rosen and Joel Weishaus; illustrated by Arthur Okamura.
    p. cm.
Includes bibliographical references.
ISBN 1-55643-530-4 (pbk.)
    1. Haiku, American. 2. Friendship—Poetry. 3. Healing—Poetry. 4. Nature—Poetry.
I. Weishaus, Joel, 1939– II. Okamura, Arthur. III. Title.
    PS3618.O8313H43 2004
    811'.608—dc22

                                                              CIP
                                                        2004007817

            1 2 3 4 5 6 7 8 9 DATA 08 07 06 05 04

For my daughter Laura, who knows that *Nature*
and *Eros* heal the soul.
—David Rosen

In memory of my parents.
—Joel Weishaus

Healing is "the intuitive art of wooing Nature."
—W.H. AUDEN[1]
(QUOTING HIS PHYSICIAN FATHER)

Haiku is humanized Nature.
—R.H. BLYTH[2]

Listen to ordinary things. Poetry is natural: a language of simplicity that takes us to the heart. It springs forth from a deep spiritual place and carries meaning.
—NAOMI SHIHAB NYE[3]

Contents

List of Illustrations

(of the Authors' Haiku)

by Arthur Okamura

who describes these monoprints as an extension of the books he did on *Bashō* and *Issa* with Robert Bly and *Oxherding* with Joel Weishaus.[4]

Acknowledgments

Heartfelt thanks to the following individuals for their support, love, friendship, and inspiration: My mother and father, Barbara and Max Rosen; Aunt Martha Middendorf; daughters Sarah (her husband Allan and my grandsons Aidan and Ben), Laura, and Rachel; brother Bill and sisters Janet, Marti, and Nancy and their families; Linda Spielman, Alice Tomoye Kumagai; Lolly Torbet; Karil and Shannon Rauss; Armin (Minu) Schmidt and Katrin Häusler; Diane Walsh; Anthony Stevens; Stipe Mestrovic; William Hamilton; AI; Katsuhiro Oimatsu and Miyuki; Hayao Kawai; Osamu Kuramitsu and Kaoru; Masashi Kushizaki and Yukiyo Uenishi; Tamae Okada, Kazuhiko Higuchi; Rika (Sato), Tatsuhiko, and Kaori Tanaka; Baofeng Feng and Yuanhong Ji; Roberto Gambini; Clarissa Pinkola Estés; Tamotsu Sakaki, Sonoko Toyoda; and Alex Tritsibidas. Many thanks to these readers for their comments and suggestions: Nathan Mascaro, Barbara Gastel, Marti Olesen, Polly Young-Eisendrath, Sam Black, Linda Spielman, Stipe Mestrovic, Charlene Broudy, Ned Leavitt, Kathi Appelt, Leslie Strickland, William Hamilton, and Cindy Boyd. I also deeply thank these three haiku masters who taught me so much with kindness and unselfish generosity: the late Robert Spiess, Ayako Isayama, and Nagayama Aya. In addition, I sincerely thank another haiku master, Joel Weishaus, for his friendship and healing spirit before, during, and after writing this book. A generous thanks to Arthur Okamura for his extraordinary yet simple illustrations. Furthermore, I deeply thank Jillian Somers and Anne Deuermeyer (who did the most) for their superb clerical and editorial skills. Finally, I thank Richard Grossinger and Lindy Hough (founders and co-publishers) and Brooke Warner (project editor) at North Atlantic Books.

—D.R.

To my family and friends, and lovers who stood by me, I can never thank you enough. To the many teachers with whom I've been blessed. To David Rosen, friend, healer, and poet. To my Dharma brother, Arthur Okamura. I also join in thanking those who have been named above.

—J.W.

Preface

ORIGINALLY KNOWN AS *hokku, haiku* was the first link in a chain of short poems, called *renga*. These linked, interactive verses were a sort of conversation between fellow poets and friends. Haiku are composed of 17 syllables, traditionally in a 5-7-5 sequence.[5] Bashō[6] is considered the first haiku master. Usually haiku are related to one of the four seasons and characterized by the following: egolessness, aloneness, acceptance, universality, humor, silence, awakening, compassion, and death.[7] While it is true that haiku maintains a dialogical quality with Nature, the human aspect has been down played except in *senryu*[8] and modern versions of renga. Since healing involves both non-personal and personal aspects, Joel and I have focused on both inter-reactive realms. In part, it speaks to our over thirty-year-old friendship. But it also concerns the healing relationship[9] and the need to react to and relate with other human beings as well as Nature.

I've been writing haiku for a quarter of a century. However, my desire to understand its psychology, meaning, and healing value is relatively recent. During an extended stay in Japan in 1999, I met Nagayama Aya, a haiku poet who was to be the co-author of this book. However, with my support and encouragement, and due to a number of life circumstances, she decided to write her own book of haiku.[10] So I set out to write this book alone. Then, while in Portland, Oregon, in 2001, giving a lecture on a previous book,[11] I met with a dear friend and poet, Joel Weishaus, who had recently moved there after spending twenty-three years in New Mexico. While talking about our various writing projects, Joel said, "It's time for us to do a book together." After exploring why and what kind of book, I

1

conveyed that this volume was a natural one for our collaboration. Born out of synchronicity, it makes perfect sense. We both write haiku and know about the interconnections of haiku with Zen Buddhism, Shintoism, and Taoism. Finally, we have both lived and traveled in Japan, absorbing the healing spirit of haiku.

Haiku fits well with Carl Jung's psychotherapeutic technique of active imagination in which meditation leads to setting ego aside so the unconscious can emerge and be integrated with the conscious in a transcendent function resulting in an artistic product.[12] Creative haiku represent a healing union of intuition and sensation, past and present, self and other, ordinary and extraordinary, as well as current and ancient memories. Haiku also produces an archetypal and affective image out of a few words.

This volume is a *haibun*[13] of the psyche, that is, a journey into Spirit and Nature. In part it is also a *haiga*[14] of the soul, as many haiku are accompanied by Arthur Okamura's distinctive drawings. There is prose about periods of melancholy that I've suffered and the healing haiku that resulted. In addition, it records moments of joy and peace that I've experienced. Joel reacts and responds to what I've written with his own healing prose and haiku. Hence, we model for the reader how to use this book and illustrate the dialogical or interactive qualities of haiku that are so healing. While it concerns what Haruo Shirane calls "the difficulty of the spiritual journey 'within,'"[15] it likewise involves sharing and "the expectation of a poetic reply."[16] We follow Bashō's poetics of "awakening to the high, returning to the low"[17] as well as the spirit of "going and returning."[18]

This is not a book about the history of haiku[19] or how to write them.[20] This is not a self-help book in the usual sense, but rather a non-self (beyond the ego) healing volume that ideally helps one to realize that we are alone,[21] yet inter-connected. This book values

"haiku moments [and] following the Creative."[22] It also underscores
the philosophy: "Moments, moments, that is life."[23]
—DAVID ROSEN
COLLEGE STATION, TEXAS

Recently, I was reading the experiences of the American Zen Master,
Robert Aiken. He told how during World War II he had been interned
in a prison camp in Japan, where a guard gave him a copy of R.H.
Blyth's *Zen in English Literature and Oriental Classics*. Later, when all
the internment camps in Kobe were combined, Aiken and Blyth met,
and became life-long friends. This returned me to San Francisco, 1968.
I was sharing a large flat with the poet William Witherup. I had the
privacy of a whole section that was formerly the servants' quarters.
My rooms overlooked a garden. It was winter, raining much of the
time, and I had the flu. That week I read R.H. Blyth's book on Zen in
English Literature, and then began to read his extensive translations of
haiku. The spirit in which these poems were written began a process
of healing in me that continues to this day. We are always beginning,
sometimes unconsciously, something, and getting over something else.
This is the process of life. After I was well enough to go outside, I spent
many days walking in Golden Gate Park, writing haiku.

In the Spring of 2002, David Rosen visited Portland to give a talk
on "The Healing Spirit of Haiku" to Oregon Friends of C.G. Jung.
One afternoon we were strolling and catching up on each other's life.
David asked how I first became interested in haiku. I told part of the
above story, and how I had written perhaps hundreds of poems that
winter, but kept only one. "Which one?," he asked:

Empty bench—

Rain

Sits down

Empty bench—

Rain

Sits down

When we speak of healing, we are not concerned with overcoming illness but of becoming whole. "Heal" and "whole" share the same etymological roots. Western medicine is in the business of patching up patients, working to keep them alive until they are beyond all of modern medicine's extraordinary means of repair. If the patient dies, the physician often feels the loss as a personal failure. Although such medicine is a necessary and noble task, it's what the practice came to be, not what it set out to become. Addressing shamanism, the longest unbroken tradition of healing, dating back to the early days of human culture, Jeanne Achterberg says: "First and foremost, avoiding death is not the purpose for the practice of medicine in the shamanic traditions. Our Western mistrust of these systems often comes from the observation that shamanic healing may not have resulted in an extension of life."[24] Here, dying is not to be taken in the mundane sense, but in what David Rosen has termed "egocide... a sacrifice of the ego to the Self, a higher principle,"[25] which is related to the Buddhist notion of "emptiness," the cauldron in which all phenomena are created, and to which they return. Compounded of wholeness (healing) and emptiness (non-being/ being), every haiku is a prescription for a larger life.

—Joel Weishaus
Portland, Oregon

A NOTE TO THE READER

This book, a haibun of the psyche, is divided into fifty-three sections concerning specific themes connected with our own healing journeys. You can go to a certain part, if you like, or read it the way it was written, as an unfolding process. It is more psychological and philosophical than logical, as the writing, like our daily lives, is unwittingly shaped by what C.G. Jung called the "collective unconscious." Subjects and places aren't as important as the depth of feelings between people who have experienced them in unexpected subtle ways. Overall, when you are finished reading this book, we trust that your view of self, of the world, and of reality itself will have changed, as ours did while writing it.

—DAVID ROSEN AND JOEL WEISHAUS

Haibun of the Psyche

You can only go halfway into the darkest forest;
then you are coming out the other side.
—Chinese Proverb[26]

1

Being Alone

DAVID:

After trudging through a harsh early mid-life crisis and a winter of much darkness and despair, in the Spring of 1978 I wrote my first haiku as an adult.[27] I was alone on a rock overlooking the Georgian Bay in Ontario, Canada. I'd been on a personal retreat in a remote place following an academic conference in Toronto. I'd awakened too soon, when the birds started to sing. I threw on some clothes and ventured out on a path I knew well. I arrived at the stone precipice thirty minutes before the sun came up above the distant line separating the blue-black water from the peach-rose sky. I sat down and meditated, then got out a small tablet to make a sketch. To my surprise, I wrote the words below, creating another kind of image. I'm not sure why this happened. It may have been, in part, the fertile soil of my depression and the sense of emptiness I felt. Regardless as to why a haiku emerged at that moment, I'm grateful that this creative process has never ceased. For a moment the emptiness became enlightenment; like drawing and painting, haiku is an activity that heals my soul.[28]

> Dawn on a spring sea—
> Then a glittering
> From a thousand jumping fish[29]

JOEL:

With the ending of a relationship, I had to reacquaint myself with the notion of once again living alone. I was feeling lonely, something unthinkable when I was younger, when the desire to be alone with myself was almost a way of life. But with age, loneliness makes its presence palpable. I suspect this is because one's psyche becomes aware of the Void over which someday it will either leap or be pushed, with no hand to hold, just myths and theories that there is an "other side." As it must be faced alone, one seeks the warmth of companionship, before that fateful moment arrives.

> In the dark bedroom,
> I close my eyes
> And wonder why

Dawn on a spring sea—
Then a glittering
From a thousand jumping fish

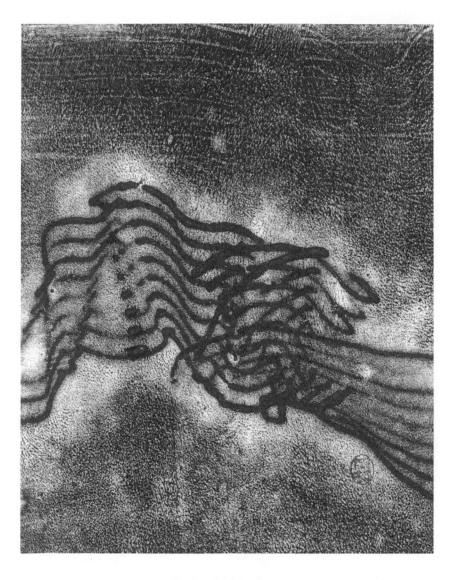

In the dark bedroom,
I close my eyes
And wonder why

2

Feeling Death

Darkness within darkness.
The gateway to all understanding.
—Lao Tzu[30]

DAVID:

In early 1994, I was by myself, on sabbatical in Zürich, Switzerland, researching and writing a book on Jung.[31] Soon after arriving in Switzerland, I was suffering from melancholy due to years of marital strife. I felt like I was dying in my half-Asian, half-Swiss apartment in the village of Bassersdorf. Prophetic of a coming transformation, my deadening writer's block ended when tears started flowing while I walked on a wooded path by a stream. All forms of water, whether rivers or tides, are healing.

> Out of darkness
> A flowing brook
> Pierces winter's silence[32]

JOEL:

One Autumn many years ago, I was living in a dilapidated farmhouse in the mountains northwest of Tokyo, with a small charcoal fire for heat. One night, I felt like I was burning up with fever, along with having a terrible headache. I believed I was going to die, an Unknown *Gaijin* in a foreign land. I got through the night scribbling in my notebook what I believed would be the last words I would ever write, trying to stay awake, convinced that if I fell asleep I wouldn't wake up.

Then, slowly, the sky brightened with bleak light. The fever was gone, the headache too. But by early afternoon they had returned. I knew I couldn't survive another night, and made quick preparations to leave. After patiently cleaning the rooms, I walked down the road to the bus stop in town.

> Head throbbing,
> A thin thread of light
> Guides me home

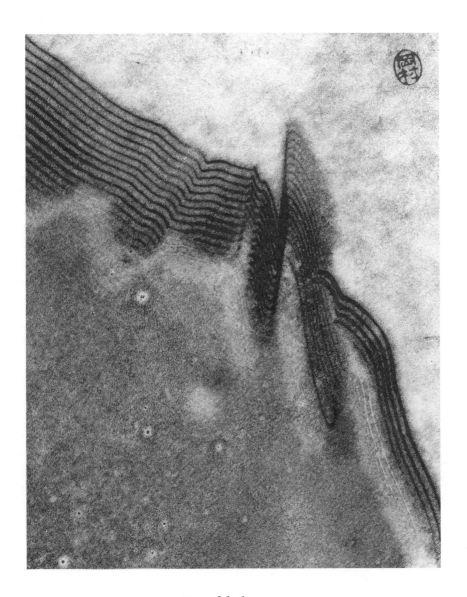

Out of darkness
A flowing brook
Pierces winter's silence

3
Dark and Light

David:

In the late afternoon, I would venture out for my daily *wanderweg,* a walk in Switzerland's countryside. I felt like Henry David Thoreau who said that walking in "...Nature, for absolute freedom and wildness..." involves "...the grace of God..." and preserves one's "...health and spirits..." Thoreau felt "...equally at home everywhere."[33] For me, these walks were creative meditations, which often resulted in healing haiku. Solidly in springtime, dark *yin* gave birth to *yang* light.

> Dark evergreen woods—
> Blossoming pear trees emerge
> In the evening light[34]

JOEL:

Four A.M. Guard Duty, somewhere in the wilds of Ft. Devens, Massachusetts. A rifle slung over my shoulder, bitter cold biting through boots, I paced up and back beneath a canopy of blinking stars, crisp sound of snow crunching underfoot, my eyes were begging to close. With moonlight framing thin black trees, "What am I guarding?" I thought. "The war's inside myself."

> Light and shadow,
> Shadow and light,
> I cross both paths

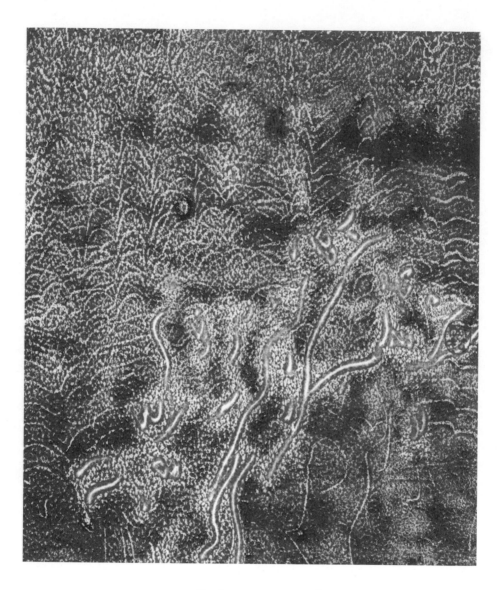

Dark evergreen woods—
Blossoming pear trees emerge
In the evening light

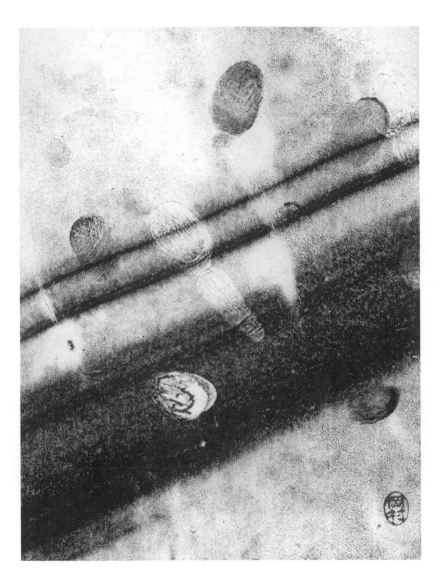

Light and shadow,
Shadow and light,
I cross both paths

4
Going to the Opposite

DAVID:

Heraclitus was right about his concept of *enantiodromia,* in which everything goes to the opposite. Often it seems sudden, but actually it proceeds with dramatic changes after long gestation periods:

> Overnight
> A yellow field of mustard
> Beyond the quiet stream[35]

> Fiery clouds
> Over a red barn—
> Green apples turning[36]

> A field of deep grass—
> Its vibrant eruption
> Of orange-red poppies[37]

JOEL:

Taoist scholar Chang Chung-yuan comments on a passage from the *Tao Te Ching* by stating that the Tao is "the unity of multiplicities as well as the unity of opposites. As the unity of multiplicities, *Tao* cannot be dominated by any of its parts . . ."[38]

> Soft red petals,
> Sharp teeth beneath—
> Rose smells so sweet

"As the unity of opposites, *Tao* produces 'the dew of peace.'"[39]

> Early morning—
> As brown leaves fall,
> Green leaves glisten

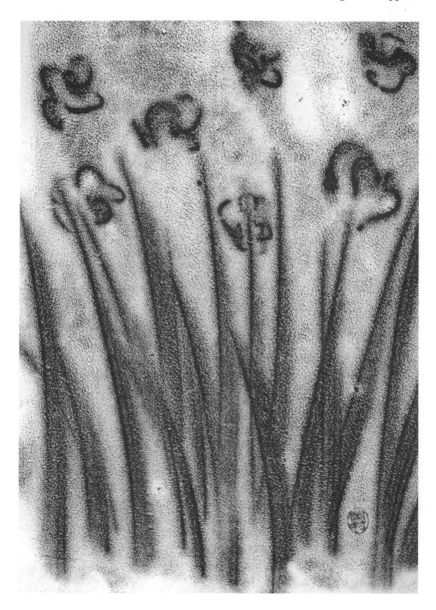

A field of deep grass—
Its vibrant eruption
Of orange-red poppies

5
Flexibility of the Spirit

David:

By late summer, work on a writing project had come to fruition. A ripening and flexibility had also transpired in my healing process. As Chris Van Cleave said, "We harvest fields we planted once knowing grains of truth would soon come to a head."[40]

> Golden wheat kernels
> Catching light of day
> Bending all ways in the wind[41]

JOEL:

In its pejorative sense, healing pertains to the body about which we spend so much of our life worrying, grooming, fighting off diseases, signs of aging, and the thought of inevitable death and decay. Even though with a healthy lifestyle, and proper medical treatment, we may prolong our life, aging and death are still inevitable.

In Taoism, so-called Immortals, I suggest, didn't live any longer than their countrymen, but were no longer *attached* to the linear birth/life/ death process. They were able, instead, to bend "all ways in the wind." In depth, this is also what the practice of yogic *asanas* is about, as are shamanic journeying postures: a flexibility of the spirit, a lightness of being.[42]

> Bird lands,
> Prances around,
> Takes off again

Golden wheat kernels
Catching light of day
Bending all ways in the wind

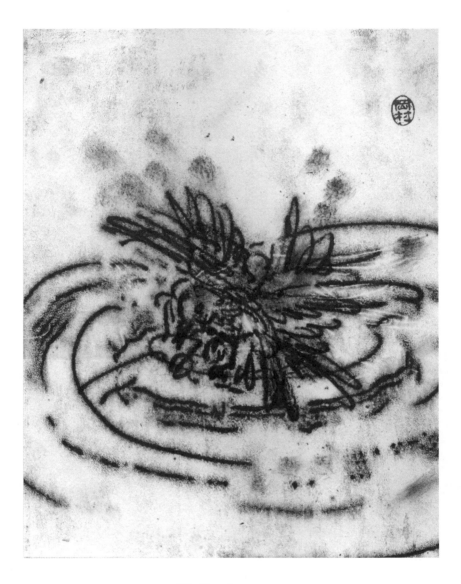

Bird lands,
Prances around,
Takes off again

6

Creative Solitude

DAVID:

Looking back, it must have been synchronicity when I read Bashō (during my 1994 stay in Switzerland) and discovered that one of his students was named Rosen.[43] This experience and the visit of Japan's first Jungian analyst, Professor Hayao Kawai, to Texas A&M University to give the 1995 Fay Lecture Series in Analytical Psychology,[44] rekindled a childhood dream of going to Japan. Subsequently, Kawai invited me to speak at a Conference in Japan during the summer of 1997. It felt uncanny: I had come home. The peace I experienced drew me back to Japan for my next sabbatical in the late summer, fall, and early winter of 1999. I was invited by Kazuhiko Higuchi to be a visiting professor at Kyoto Bunkyo University, a small Buddhist university in Uji City, in the southern part of Kyoto. My research involved understanding the psychology of haiku, its meaning and healing value.

Two nights before I left Texas for Japan, I had this dream: I said to an Asian woman, "What you create by writing holds peace for your father." This woman in the dream looked like a Taoist monk at the White Cloud Monastery in Beijing, whom I'd met during a trip to China in December of 1998. From a rural village, she planned to return there as a priest after two years of training. I interpreted the Taoist dream-woman as my inner muse and haiku poet. I didn't realize how prophetic the dream was until a month later. I didn't know then that a large part of my time in Japan would bring peace to my father's soul and to my own.[45]

The initial haiku I wrote in Japan came to me following the departure of my three daughters, who had been with me on holiday during my first two weeks there. Being alone after a loss allows for healing (a process toward wholeness) to occur. The extraordinary, yet ordinary, event I wrote about was experienced on the grounds of the Buddhist university where I worked. As I was leaving to go home, I stopped by a fish pond and noticed that the *koi*[46] (which represent transformation) made a moving circle or mandala, which symbolizes spiritual wholeness. I felt centered and this was mirrored in the full moon (a symbol of the Tao and its matriarchal origin).

> Ring of moving koi
> In misty reflecting pool—
> Full moon at sunset

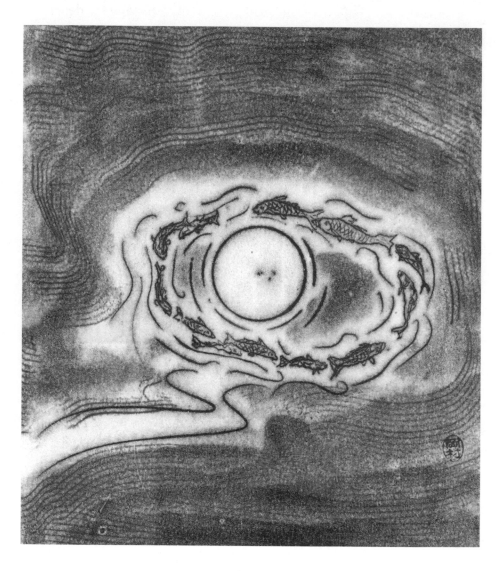

Ring of moving koi
In misty reflecting pool—
Full moon at sunset

JOEL:

Maurice Blanchot quotes from a letter by the poet Rainer Maria Rilke: "my solitude has finally closed in and I am contained in my work like a kernel in its fruit." Blanchot also says that Rilke "refers to a solitude which is not essentially solitude but rather self-communication."[47] He is reminding us that it is only with such a sense of solitude as Rilke described that we can reach the center of our unfolding. But creative solitude and relationship with the world are not two.

One evening, in our farmhouse northwest of Tokyo, a neighbor joined us for dinner, smiling as he graciously struggled with his few words of English—

> Warming his teeth
> Over foreign words,
> "Ah, so, fish, eat."

7
Death of the Ego

DAVID:

Being alone also shows its dark side as when part of my ego died[48] and became creatively transformed while in Japan. This is similar to Natsume Sōseki's goal of egolessness (*muga*) and his ultimate objective of "following heaven, leaving self (*sokuten kyoshi*)."[49]

> Facing death
> Cicada and I
> Sing the same song[50]

This haiku by Issa gave me comfort:

> Live in simple faith
> Just as this trusting cherry
> Flowers, fades, and falls[51]

JOEL:

Hayao Kawai wrote that, "It is rather threatening for a Japanese to encounter the Western ego, which is developed as an independent entity, as if utterly distant from all that is not 'I' (i.e., everything else). The Japanese presuppose a connection—with others, with all else, in the sense of oneness."[52]

   This is a barrier that faces many Western students of Zen, as their "independent entity," the mind that's been developing over most of their life, is difficult to drop, if only for a moment. Understanding this is what led many Japanese Zen Masters to refuse to train Westerners. And even though there is now a cadre of authorized Western Zen Masters, this ego, grounded in one's culture, is still a problem that, perhaps, never will be satisfactorily resolved.

> Sudden storm—
>
> Roots sit
>
> In the air

8
Learning to Bow

DAVID:

I am 6 feet 4 inches tall. So when I got to Japan, where most people are a foot shorter, I kept hitting my head, especially on door frames. The psychology and meaning of the following humorous haiku, or more accurately senryu, is that I was being humbled in Japan as my ego was being knocked around. Humor, connected to the spirit, involves the ability of not taking oneself too seriously and this is healing.

> Too tall
> Head knocked silly—
> Learning to bow[53]

Regarding how someone liberates his own being, Lao Tzu said, "He does this not by elevating himself, but by lowering himself."[54]

JOEL:

An Hasidic Rabbi said, "One must lower oneself, in order to raise oneself." In this spirit, the "crawl-in passage," *nijiri-guchi,* the entrance of a traditional Japanese tea room is only thirty-six inches high. It is designed this way so that each guest, regardless of social position, must lower themselves an equal distance. However, like in most societies, some Japanese are more equal than others; so there is also a *kinin-guchi,* a "walk-in passage," through which "special guests" can enter standing up.

> Standing up fast,
>
> My head
>
> spins

On a less civilized note: Addressing the relationship between predator and prey, Anthony Weston suggests that domesticated animals, such as cows and sheep, are attacked by wolves because they have lost their ability to signal their selfhood to the predator. What Barry Lopez calls "the conversation of death" has been bred out of them. Inversely, Weston says, humans must relearn how to bow "before the mysteries of the world, entering a kind of wild etiquette."[55]

> Stomach growls—
>
> Bear tracks
>
> In the mud

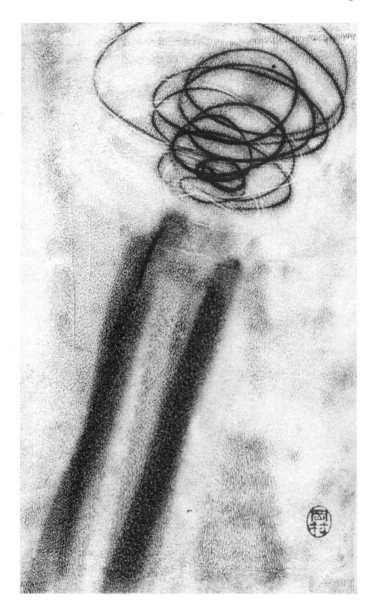

Standing up fast,

My head

spins

9
Wise Old Women

DAVID:

The haiku below was written after visiting Ayako Isayama, a wise old Japanese woman, who was also a haiku poet. She lived in a spiritual community in Kyoto called ITTOEN. Ayako had given up everything (egolessness) to join a monastic way of life. And this life style had drawn her closer to the divine mystery of Nature. We sat in her tranquil room looking outside while we drank green tea together. I wrote the following poem for her to celebrate our meeting:

> Grasshopper on the wall—
> Through the open door
> Moonflowers in soft rain[56]

JOEL:

Every man, at certain stages of his life, needs a spiritually wise old woman as adviser. When I was in my late 20s, I visited the Zen Mountain Center at Tassajara Springs, California. One morning I met Marian Mountain. When I first saw her, besides her physical beauty, I sensed the strength of someone who had found her path and had made a full commitment to following it. However, like Thomas Merton, Marian was a monk with a hermit's soul, a contradiction that soon led to her being asked to leave the monastery. She found a cabin nearby, where "The east wall of the Pacific Ocean beat on the west wall of the Santa Lucias. . . . Many mornings I sat enveloped in cool clouds that drifted in and out of the small hut I named Half-Dipper Hermitage."[57]

During the next ten years, Marian married again, moved to Idaho, and wrote a well-received book on Zen. We remained in touch, exchanging letters, in which she guided me through some harrowing psycho-spiritual times.

More recently, I met an elderly woman from Kiev, the same city from which my mother's parents fled a century ago. This woman and I had several interesting conversations; and when she suddenly died, not long after we met, my loss was profound.

> Silent at her funeral—
> We had spoken only
> A few days ago

10

Walking the Countryside

DAVID:

Each day I would leave my tiny apartment in Mukaijima and walk about three miles. Within five minutes I'd be in the countryside with fields of green tea plants and rice paddies.

> Shimmering paddy—
> The slap of small feet nearing
> Where dragonflies hover[58]

JOEL:

At Numata, near the Japanese Alps, rice farmers looked up from their work to wave. I leaped ditches and walked the edges of furrows to a shrine marked off with strips of fluttering white paper and a broken stone lantern.

> Holding an unlit lantern,
> The Buddha enlightened
> His ancestors too

Shimmering paddy—
The slap of small feet nearing
Where dragonflies hover

11

Making Peace with One's Father

DAVID:

During August the *Bon* festival takes place. Soen Nakagawa said that
". . . *Bon* (the Day of the Dead) or *Urabon,* which came from *ullam-
bana* in Sanskrit, means being hung upside down."[59] It is a time when
you pray for your ancestors' souls. Two Japanese friends, Masashi
Kushizaki and Yukiyo Uenishi, took me to a Buddhist temple where
I joined in the flow of the ritual. Since I felt that my deceased father's
soul was the most troubled, the priest recited a prayer, which he wrote
in calligraphy on a thin piece of wood. I obtained *maki* (a pine bough)
and *hozuki* (an orange lantern-shaped flower pod that is said to con-
tain the soul of the prayed for ancestor). I lit incense and bowed in
silence.

> Make peace with father
> At home create altar—
> Pray for his soul

After a week, I remembered a dream in which my father and I
embraced (something we rarely did in real life), and a sense of peace
washed over me.

JOEL:

The year after my father died, on his birthday, I drove to the foothills of the Sandia Mountains, at the eastern edge of Albuquerque. It was strangely wet and cold for May. Only one other car was in the parking lot, a man there to walk his dog. I waited until they left before leaving the car.

Wanting to gain some height, I walked to the nearest mesa and climbed, looking for a spot out of the wind and rain. In a half-sheltered place, walls covered with graffiti, floor littered with empty beer cans, I set up a small altar and lit a stick of incense in honor of my father. Wind howled between the rocks, rain threatened to douse the stick's tiny red eye. Huddled in my patched down jacket, which had kept me warm during many backpacking trips, I thanked my father for the love and support he had given me, especially when he didn't understand or approve of my path, so different from his.

> Howling wind, droning rain—
> Who's speaking?
> Who's listening?

12

Nuclear Darkness

DAVID:

Visiting the Atomic-Bomb Dome, Memorial Peace Park, Eternal Flame, and the Museum in Hiroshima was an upsetting, yet profound experience. The grey sky and quiet rain set the mood. In the Peace Park Museum there is a piece of a wall that was in front of a bank near the epicenter of the blast. When the Atomic bomb exploded, a man was sitting in front of this segment of the wall; all that remained was his shadow. That night I couldn't sleep; I was haunted by the souls of the 140,000 people killed (mostly women and children). I felt shame at being human.

> Shadow burnt into wall—
> Rain falls, leaving no sound
> Behind[60]

JOEL:

Although I didn't visit Hiroshima, in New Mexico I spent several years researching and writing about the extensive nuclear infrastructure that remains in that state where the two bombs that were exploded over Japan were designed and built.[61]

> Never before,
>
> Such sour
>
> Green rocks[62]

What seems telling is that six decades after the destruction of Hiroshima and Nagasaki, the earth is still soured with nuclear weaponry. Before the first bomb was built at Los Alamos, the concern of some physicists was that once the genie is out of the bottle he can't be put back in. The genie is technology, and the bottle is the human psyche.

This is not a problem of whether or not to advance knowledge, as the human thirst for knowledge is unquenchable. The problem is not scientific, but philosophical: What is security?

> Independence Day—
>
> With bangs and bursts
>
> Stars are blotted out

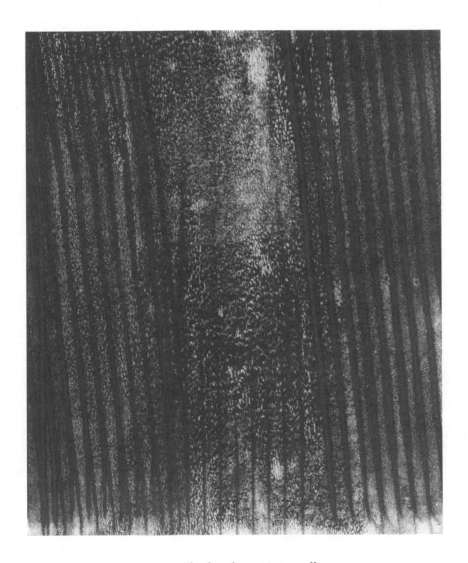

Shadow burnt into wall—
Rain falls, leaving no sound
Behind

13
Seeing the Mountain

DAVID:

A calm came over me when I visited Shirakawa Gassho Mura, an old and simple village in the Alpine region of Japan. I ventured up into the forest on a narrow path and came to a clearing. I looked back at this verdant place.

> Village of thatched roofs
> On a lush mountain
> The monk's meal of greens[63]

Later:

> Bright sun—
> Sound of wind
> Rippling through bamboo[64]

JOEL:

One day I climbed the hill behind Ryutaku-ji[65] to get a good view of Mt. Fuji. What I remember seeing, however, was an outhouse and wondering what it was doing there.

The holy mountain, with its pure white crown, was juxtaposed with a smelly shithouse. The volcano boiling Earth's hot entrails, and a man squatting over a hole in the ground.

> Bow to the trees,
>
> Bow to the leaves—
>
> Autumn's lesson

When I returned to the monastery, it was silent, but for the soft patter of raindrops. Like Paradise, it was too perfect.

> What does one do
>
> In Eden?
>
> Get out!

Bow to the trees,
Bow to the leaves—
Autumn's lesson

14
Bashō's Journey

DAVID:

I went to Nikko following Bashō's account of his journey north.[66] I recalled his words, "What is important is to keep our mind high in the world of true understanding, and returning to the world of our daily experience to seek therein the truth of beauty."[67] It seemed miraculous that it was still the same and such an awesome sacred site. Even though depressed, I felt better.

> Golden gate—
> *Sugi* trees reaching
> Light in the abyss[68]

JOEL:

Bashō was always leaving home, always entering a liminal state, each journey an initiation, a deepening of insight, poetry, and wit. There he is in his tiny house preparing for another long walking tour, thinking, "This journey will be my last." Feeling his age, he packed light, burdened only by the presents friends piled on him, which he was too polite to refuse, and his death, which he carried like an altar.

> Bashō's thin legs
> Carried everything
> needed

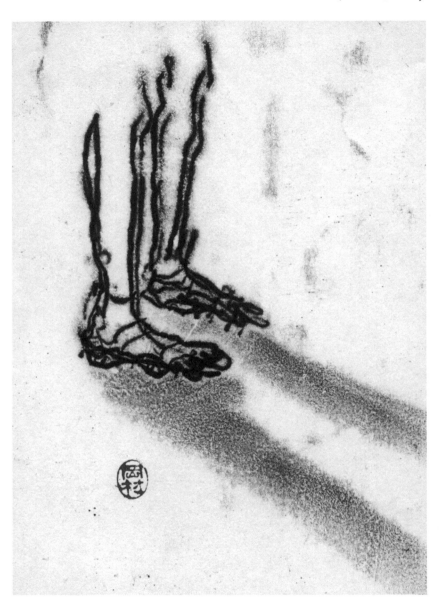

Bashō's thin legs
Carried everything
            needed

15
Some Snapshots of Japan

DAVID:

Back in my small apartment in Mukaijima where I ate soba and drank green tea:

Fresh cut flowers—
I sit and wonder
Who's dying?[69]

Can't sleep
No reason why, no reason why not—
Mouse scurries across floor[70]

Then as the sun comes up:

Arms raised
I cry "I love you!"—
No sound comes out

The next day a typhoon whips through Kyoto.

Thunder, lightning
Horizontal rain—
Washing dishes very slowly[71]

JOEL:

When I returned to San Francisco, working my way back in the greasy belly of an old oil tanker, having been gone about three months, I had breakfast with my friend Jay Stattman.[72] Over a breakfast of scrambled eggs, he told me that his girlfriend had just died in a car accident. Then he suddenly realized, "You've been in Japan! I want to hear all about it. But not today." He never mentioned Japan again.

> Today dark clouds
> Nudge the sun:
> *Dream*

16

Dreaming

*A dream is like a butterfly which happens
to fly into my garden.
I can see and appreciate it, but the butterfly comes
and goes of its own accord.*
—Hayao Kawai[73]

David:

Only once has a haiku come to me in a dream. I'd just met Nagayama
Aya, my Japanese haiku poet friend, who is in the *Hototogisu*[74] School
of Haiku. The next morning I woke up from a sound sleep and wrote
down this poem:

> Fireflies light the way
>
> Lonely haiku hut—
>
> Hototogisu calls

JOEL:

It is very rare to wake up and continue a poem begun in a dream. Usually, it doesn't make sense, or is shallow, like how extraordinary insights gained while high on a psychotropic drug may seem mundane in midst of ordinary life. Because it was a "sound sleep," one that invited sound, the poem wasn't written, but spoken. If it had been written, where would it be when the dreamer woke up? This is the same question the poet Samuel Coleridge asked, although he had a flower in mind.[75] In both cases, the dreamer has tapped into a world in which magic is ordinary.

> This morning
> The bird's song
> Suddenly makes sense!

Fireflies light the way
Lonely haiku hut—
Hototogisu calls

17
Facing Reality

DAVID:

I leave my humble abode:

> After a sudden storm—
> Walking on a carpet
> Of white petals

Soon I witness evidence of the bursting of the Japanese economic bubble.

> Under a bridge
> Pigeon droppings everywhere
> Homeless people stare

On the way back:

> Autumn wind—
> First red leaf
> In muddy pool

JOEL:

When we walk outside, it is like when Prince Siddhartha, the future Buddha, left the palace and took a stroll, much to the chagrin of his parents, who had carefully sheltered him from the realities of life. Along the way, he came upon an old man dying by the roadside. Realizing that this condition was in his path too, that old age and death are as unavoidable as breathing, no matter what one's wealth or rank in society, the young man was shaken to his roots.

> On the pavement—
> Fallen soggy leaves
> Unable to go home

18
Eating

DAVID:

A confession: During my stay in Japan, there were times when I
craved a non-Japanese breakfast, so I'd go to a Western restaurant.
On this particular day, a Buddhist funeral procession passed in front
of my eyes.

> As I eat pancakes,
> Mourners pass by—
> Life, too, is round

JOEL:

In Kyoto, in the windows of restaurants that offer Western food, there are replicas of the food offered on the menu, so that customers who cannot read Japanese can point to what they want. These plastic hamburgers and such looked so unappetizing, tasteless, and indigestible, that I opted for Japanese cuisine. Over a period of time, I was left so constipated from the starchy food that I feared for my life.

> There's no way
> Around it, noodles
> For dinner tonight

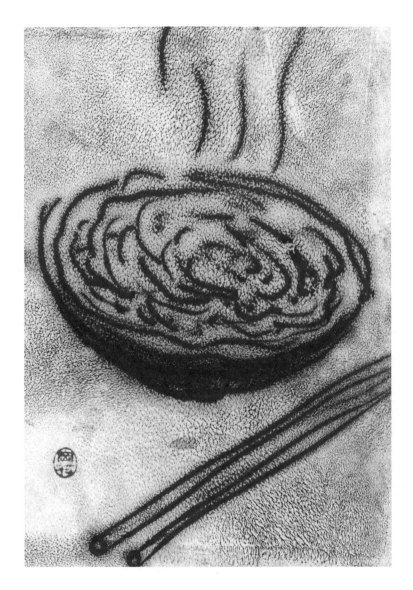

There's no way
Around it, noodles
For dinner tonight

19
Ikebana

DAVID:

On my little balcony the morning after my first *Ikebana*[76] class, which I loved!

> Eyes shut,
> Warm sun on my face—
> As if a bud were about to open

I thought of Onitsura's haiku:

> Silent flowers
> Speak also
> To that obedient ear within[77]

JOEL:

While the Hebrew God gave humans dominion over the planet, Buddhists have always paid humble tribute to Nature's "incredible wisdom."[78]

In the sixth century, Japanese devotees brought offerings of cut flowers to Buddhist temples, a practice that evolved into arrangements called *rikka*, "standing flowers," that symbolically represented various Buddhist motifs.

By the late sixteenth century, the simpler style of *nageire*, "to throw, or toss, in," was preferred, complementing the precise and austere rituals, such as the tea ceremony, that had come into vogue, and the *tokonoma*, or alcove, in which calligraphic art and flowers were displayed in private homes.

In the 1890s, as Japan opened to the West, the *moribana*, "piled-up flowers," school of Ikebana was introduced. With a bow toward the less formal approaches of the West, *moribana* is an accessible style that concentrates the healing power of a garden scene into a vase of stems, leaves, flowers, and buds.

A tiny myth, a fantasy, a journey focused with imagination:

> In the vase, climbers
> On a distant peak—
> Ants?

20

Honoring Old Age

DAVID:

One of my trips was to the southernmost island of Kyushu, where I was to give lectures at a psychiatric hospital and Kyushu University in Fukuoka. As I was leaving, I had an instructive beginning to the journey. I was relearning to honor the elderly and to be patient.

> Dragging my suitcase,
> An old lady cycles past—
> Crows circling above

> Old couple shuffles along,
> Heads bent under black hats—
> I miss my train

While in Kyushu, I visited Noike (Sacred Pond) near Mt. Aso with my friends Rika Sato-Tanaka, Tatsuhiko Tanaka (her husband), and Kaori (their daughter).

> Dancing light
> Yellow leaves float—
> Sound of raindrops

JOEL:

At the autumnal celebration in Tokyo of the 100TH anniversary of the Meiji Restoration, which, in 1868, restored power to the Emperor, moving the capitol from Kyoto to Tokyo, ancient-looking masters of the Martial Arts demonstrated their moves, limbs stiff but proud. One small man with a wispy beard, thick wrists, and a long white robe, caught my attention. Attacked from all sides by his black-belted students, without moving a muscle he sent the young men flying.

Years later, when I was an Aikido student in San Francisco, I recognized a picture of him on a wall of the dojo. He was Morihei Uyeshiba, called, O Sensei, "Honorable Teacher," the founder of Aikido. Later I learned that I had seen him give one of the last demonstrations of harmony with the universe, "The Art of Peace."

> As winter approaches,
> The old Master dons
> A white robe

Old couple shuffles along,
Heads bent under black hats—
I miss my train

21
Life in Texas

DAVID:

The fall colors are so spectacular, enchanting, and unique that the Japanese have a national holiday to go tree gazing! I felt in awe and renewed.

> Trees in Japan
> Shade
> Life in Texas

JOEL:

I had to ask directions several times. When I was finally inside, Houston's glaring sun submitted to a large cool room, impressive in size and silence. There were benches and, in the front, a single *zafu,* a meditation cushion on which a young man sat. Around the circumference of the room, Mark Rothko's fourteen paintings integrated themselves with the octagon-shaped architecture and subdued lighting. Like Matisse before him, Rothko had been given the freedom to design his own chapel,[79] this one in Texas.

Born in Latvia, in 1903, Rothko grew up in Portland, Oregon, where I often pass the high school he attended. After settling in New York City, he became one guiding light among Abstract Expressionist painters of the 1940s and 1950s.

> Beams of light streak through
> Splintered redwood stump—
> Pulp cathedral

During the last years of his life, Rothko painted works of subtle yet opaque mysteries that brought forth the dark night of his soul. Death permeates all levels of consciousness; there are no partitions. The play of the stark Texas sun[80] against the paintings' dense windows was like seeing immense pain rolled out on the walls. All around I heard a stifled cry for healing that was never answered.

> No rain for weeks—
> Crow lands, loudly
> Claiming the carrion

22

Thanksgiving Day

DAVID:

I had Thanksgiving alone in Japan. I felt nostalgic and thought about lively family gatherings. It was odd being in Uji City and thinking of American Indians, Pilgrims, and a festive turkey dinner. Feeling lonely, I took my usual walk:

> Cold wind
> Gingko leaves dance
> Golden path

JOEL:

On Thanksgiving Day, I returned from my mother's funeral, making the long trip from Ft. Lauderdale back to Portland, arriving home in time for dinner with friends. Jet-lagged, sitting in front of their fireplace, I told how, as the coffin was being lowered, a blemish on my brother-in-law's face began to bleed. Putting his hand on the wound, he said, "This is a sign from your father that his wife has joined him."[81]

> Leaves fall
> Into the waiting
> Arms of leaves

Dying at age ninety-five, Mother had been in my life for so many years, at least on the telephone, that it was difficult to comprehend her sudden absence. What could "not being here" mean? If not here, must the person be somewhere else?

There is a Zen story that has become a koan, a question that can only be answered with one's whole being. A Master and his disciple attend the funeral of a fellow monk. The Master taps on the coffin and asks, "Dead or alive?" Receiving no answer, he replies, "Neither dead nor alive."

> Sprinkling handful of earth
> Onto coffin's lid—
> Patter of rain

23
Leaving

David:

During the last days of November, I visited Soni Mura's *susuki*[82] field with Nagayama Aya and her husband Yasutaka. We went there in the day and night. The following haiku was written at midnight as the full moon was about to rise over the mountain top:

> Bitter cold—
>
> Moon light uncovers
>
> Sleeping susuki

In early December 1999, it got even colder.

> Gusts of chilly wind
>
> Leaves fly, winter is coming
>
> So is my leaving

JOEL:

Many of the best ancient Chinese poems are about leaving, as government officials, the educated class from which most of the best poets came, were frequently reposted, shifted around the country by the emperor, so they couldn't establish bases of political influence. "Another etán!" art critic and novelist John Berger wrote. "Etán, which means 'transfer' in Russian, was the word prisoners used in the Gulag when they were moved from one camp to another."[83]

David and I once discussed how leaving the home of one's childhood and adolescence in order to make a new home, one with adult responsibilities, is the first step in the journey toward Maturity. You must leave in order to arrive, give up in order to receive. Although this process is more psychological than somatic, it often means moving physically too.

> Leaf glides down
> Through morning fog—
> A train's distant whistle

24
In the Flow

DAVID:

In the early morning hours on the day I left Japan, I wrote a "death poem"[84] in memoriam of the part of me that died in Japan. My name in Kanji characters is Ro (dew) Sen (river). Buddhist literature often refers to the world as the "world of dew." Couple this with my philosophy: flow with the river of life. Hence, I re-enter the world with a new perspective on death and being.

> I flow into
>
> The world of dew—
>
> A river streaming back toward the sun

JOEL:

"A river streaming back toward the sun" brings to me an image of
Africa. Not today's continent, but as it was when our ancestors,
emerging as hominoids, lived there. Vast savannahs were the killing
fields of huge reptiles, gestating caution that rose in throats not yet
speaking sensible words, probably communicating with simple hand
signals, having learned that working together they had a better chance
to survive. Some speech-sounds, then. But the first deliberate marks
were still far in the future, in the Lower Paleolithic, where evidence
of writing has been discovered: symbolization, the phenomenon that
both ties us to, and separates us from, the objective world.

> At the end of a dream
> I awake, and realize
> I am still asleep

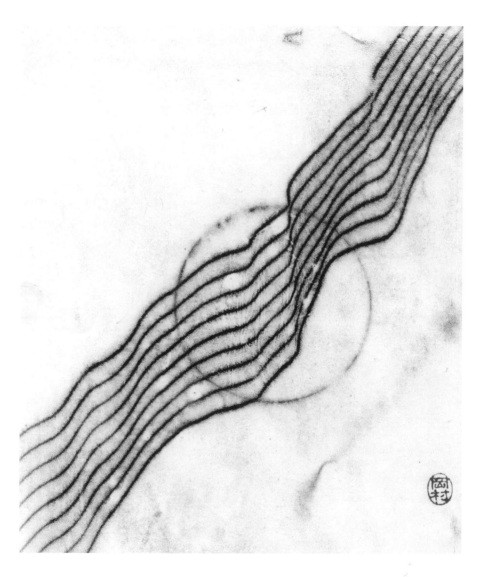

I flow into
The world of dew—
A river streaming back toward the sun

25
Anima

DAVID:

On the long plane ride home from Osaka, Japan, to Dallas, Texas, I witnessed this (perhaps heralding a growing loving relationship with my *anima*):

> Eyes closed
> Her lips full and moist
> Waiting to be kissed

JOEL:

C.G. Jung suggests that *anima* means soul, which "sometimes referred to a long generative air in the head, or soul in the breath."[85] Thus, when we are in love we feel light-headed, as if taking in too much breath. And we "soul-kiss," not only touching tongues but exchanging breath, becoming "soul-mates."

> Lips wed to leaps
> Can't pretend a poet
> Won't sacrifice speech[86]

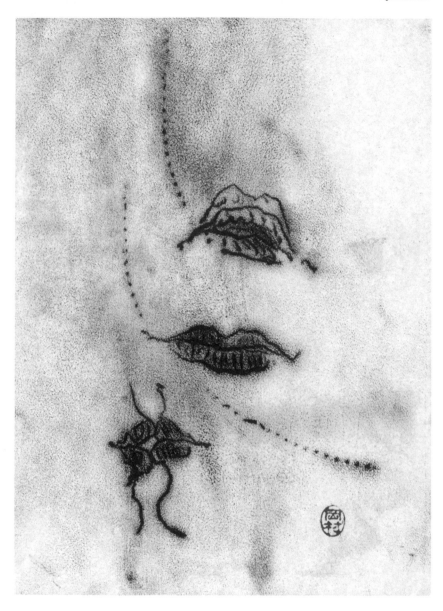

Eyes closed
Her lips full and moist
Waiting to be kissed

Lips wed to leaps
Can't pretend a poet
Won't sacrifice speech

26
Swaying Like a Tree

DAVID:

In Springfield, Missouri, in late December 1999, I celebrated the holidays and my brother Bill's New Year's Eve birthday. From the arched window in the room where I stayed on the top floor of my brother's house, I saw:

> Swaying leafless trees
> Wild geese cross silent pond—
> Awaiting the New Year

JOEL:

Met a woman on the street today who was looking up at nothing I could see. I asked her what she was looking at. She replied, "I'm looking up to the Lord, rather than looking down to the Devil." Continuing in this direction, I wondered whether the leaves of trees are atrophied wings, which took their evolutionary route when they couldn't uproot the heavy bulk of their body. Then I remembered how, standing in front of my mother's grave, chanting The Mourner's Kaddish, the rabbi swayed like a tree caught in a sudden storm; bending, yet deeply planted. For how long?

> Fallen over the path,
> Yesterday's tree stood tall—
> Yellow daisies, red eyes

27
Butterfly

What a caterpillar calls the end of the world,
[the rest of the world] calls a butterfly.
—RICHARD BACH[87]

DAVID:

Returning to my house in the Brazos Valley (which means valley of arms in Spanish), I felt a sense of calm. As promised, I wrote and sent the following haiku to my colleague and friend, Professor Sakaki in Japan, concerning a hundred-year-old beautiful painting on silk, which he had given me as a going-away gift:

> Still
> Above the blue and red flowers—
> The golden butterfly

JOEL:

One symbol for soul is butterfly. As Jung states it, "The German word *Seele* is closely related, via the Gothic form *saiwalô,* to the Greek word *αἰόλος,* which means 'quick moving,' 'changeful of hue,' 'twinkling,' something like a butterfly . . . which reels drunkenly from flower to flower and lives on honey and love."[88] A cycle of beauty pinned to the Wheel of Variegated Forms.

> Butterfly alights
> On a flower—
> Name unknown

28
The Oldest Tree in the World

DAVID:

In College Station, Texas, spring comes early. On my birthday, February 25, 2000, I wrote:

> In the sun
> Leaves bursting forth—
> I, too, feel reborn

As a gift to myself, I planted a specimen of the oldest tree in the world, which originated in China, in my front yard.

> Brazos ginkgo—
> Green leaves
> Draw up darkness

JOEL:

Planting the "oldest tree in the world" foregrounds the meaning of age. When I was young I thought age was the accumulation of birthdays. Now I think the opposite.

We are born in the wizened image of an ancient sage, new life being the opening of a forgotten wound, forgetfulness being the prelude to healing. So we purposefully become infantile, seeing ourselves as reflected in the eyes of others. As the years pass, we slowly become ourselves again: smaller, balder, wiser.

> Leaf falls,
>
> Landing on
>
> Its other side

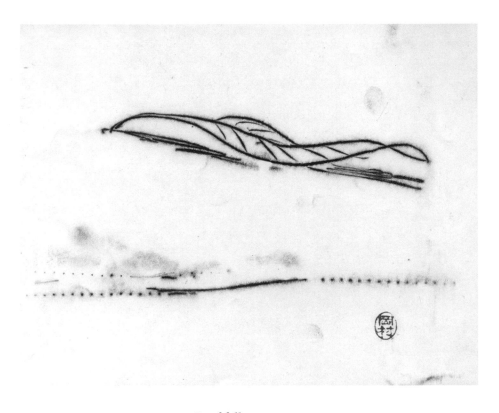

Leaf falls,
Landing on
Its other side

29
Summer Heat

DAVID:

During the late spring and early summer, it's a joy to spend time on my deck.

> Labrador puppy
> Jumps to catch a buzzing wasp
> And barely misses

> Unrelenting sun
> Bakes and burns—
> Scarlet bougainvillea blossoms

JOEL:

When I left New Mexico, driving west, I had forgotten how much of the West is desert. It was late May, 106 degrees in Las Vegas. Even after turning north, the land remained sere. It wasn't until I reached California that green prevailed; but the air remained hot and dry until I crossed into Oregon. Yet this summer is dry, even here.

> Cloudy day,
> No rain—
> Autumn's promise
>
> Mountains hidden behind clouds—
> A squirrel stares up at me,
> As if I know the future!

30
Land of Enchantment

DAVID:

During the summer of 2001, I ventured to the Abbey of Our Lady of Guadalupe in Pecos, New Mexico, for a needed retreat. I stayed in a hermitage, finished a book on the Tao,[89] walked by the river, and got closer to Nature. Thoreau was wise when he said, ". . . there is a subtle magnetism in Nature, which, if we unconsciously yield to it, will direct us aright."[90]

NATURE

Dark clouds give way to
Glowing rain-washed boulders
Sunlit spires of rock

Kneeling so low—
Eye to eye with the
Caterpillar crossing the path

Struggling black beetle
Up and over rocks
Only to start anew

PILGRIMAGE

I am
No more than flowing water
No more than sunny skies
No more than howling wind

By the river's edge
Music of the soul—
Birds sing along[91]

Walking back to the Abbey
Trees bowing to the river
I feel the same way

JOEL:

I spent my first summer in New Mexico taking care of a small ranch in Pecos. I lived in a tiny house, sleeping in the bunk upstairs. Water was hand-pumped from a well, and dinner was cooked on a Coleman stove, with an outhouse for recycling. Quiet, but for coyotes howling in the distance, the night sky was clear, the air fresh and cool.

> Alone in bed—
>
> Stars wink at each other
>
> A billion miles apart

A few years later, living in Santa Fe, I was writing the introduction and notes to a book by Thomas Merton.[92] As part of the research, I visited the Benedictine Abbey of Our Lady of Guadalupe at Pecos. There I spoke with the abbot, David Geraets, about Fr. Merton, as I had done at the Monastery of Christ in the Desert, also in New Mexico, where Merton had visited in 1968. Christ in the Desert is all male, while Our Lady of Guadalupe is co-ed. Like a trickster, I dreamed of Merton introducing erotic Tantric practices here, as he had taught Zen Buddhist meditation at Christ in the Desert, imagining attractions between the monks and nuns, with clandestine affairs unfolding in the silent desert night.

> Moon drifts past my pillow—
>
> Reaching into the darkness,
>
> Her face is wet with tears

31
September 11, 2001

DAVID:

September 11, 2001, of course, upset and depressed me. I wrote a haiku to help me and others heal; it was written in commemoration of the thousands killed in the terrorist attacks:

> Spirits rise
> From ashes; at night
> New stars glow

JOEL:

My view was different. While watching that dreadful scene played over and over again on TV, I thought about the tens of millions of people around the world who are suffering every day from violence, or wasting away from disease and malnutrition. I hoped that my country would not turn inward and mourn only itself, as now no people can heal themselves unless the entire planet, human and otherwise, is healing too.

> Sluggish creek—
> A shadow dips
> And drinks

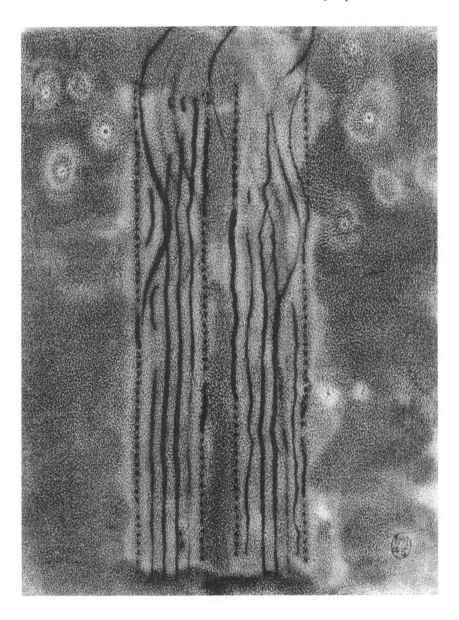

Spirits rise
From ashes; at night
New stars glow

32
Visiting Georgia

DAVID:

In the autumn of 2002, I went to the Simpsonwood Center to lead an annual retreat on "The Healing Spirit of Haiku" for the Atlanta Jung Society in Georgia. This lovely center, just outside the city, is in a large protected wilderness area with gentle forested hills that slope down to the Chattahoochee river. After an initial lecture about haiku, we all meditated and went off by ourselves in Nature to write one or more of these little poems based on what we experienced. Later everyone shared their haiku with the group. I wrote these:

> Old fallen tree
> Ferns surround its branches—
> Sound of wind

> Leaves fall
> On praying mantis—
> Autumn wind

JOEL:

In the summer of 1969, in front of the original San Francisco Zen Center, I met Patrick de Sercey.[93] Count de Sercey had been born into the French aristocracy, his family moving to the United States after World War II. Earning graduate degrees in Art History and Philosophy, he was on the faculty of Valdosta State University.

In his VW bus, Pat gave me a ride to Pacific Grove while telling me some of his story, which included peyote trips with Indians in the Southwest, and a serious dedication to the practice of Zen meditation. When we arrived at my destination, I asked for his home address, something I always did during those vagabond days.

That winter, finding myself in a frigid New York City, I decided to visit Pat's home near the Georgia/Florida border. There were two houses. In Pat's I took meals and had long conversations. In the other, which he rented to a few of his students, I slept. The latter was run down, rats scurrying in the walls, the bathtub stained orange.

> Sulfurous water—
> Cricket sings
> His dry song
>
> My new friend—
> Frog croaking
> Past midnight

33
Mother Ill, Mother Dead

DAVID:

In the winter of 2002, I traveled to Prairie Village, Kansas (a suburb of Kansas City, Missouri), to visit my mother. Snow was falling when I stopped to get some groceries on the way.

> So cold
>
> Burr—
>
> Well-to-do lady gave bag lady a ride

At the ripe old age of ninety, my mother still writes poems and makes Christmas ornaments, purses, as well as quilts. However, she is chronically ill with emphysema from years of smoking cigarettes. To her credit, at the age of sixty, she gave them up.

> Mother on oxygen
>
> Coughing—
>
> White orchid blooms

JOEL:

While my mother lay in a hospice in Ft. Lauderdale, I was on the other side of the country. At ninety-five, she had survived so many incidents that would have killed a less tenacious spirit, that her nurse told us she'd probably survive again. So my sister left her side, and a few hours later she peacefully passed away.

Shakti, my Zen priest friend, tells me she's ready to die whenever it happens. I usually am too.

> Tenaciously knocking
>
> On a dead tree—
>
> Woodpecker's empty head

In Buddhism, life and death are cognate. There is no preparation for death, except for how one lives one's everyday life. With each in-breath, I am reborn. With each out-breath, I die again. Today I notice that Shakti's shaven head reflects light like a moon.

> Moon, skull
>
> Rise, set
>
> Together

34
Scattering of Families

DAVID:

After a stop at my brother Bill's in Springfield, Missouri, for his New Year's Eve birthday, I headed further south to my sister Marti's in Ponca, Arkansas. She and her husband, Larry, co-own and operate the Lost Valley Canoe and Lodging Company. Marti, her thirteen-year-old daughter, Nonah, and I took a New Year's hike on a trail along and above the Buffalo River.

> Cold feet
> Snow flakes fall—
> Sound of beech trees in the wind

JOEL:

During the nineteenth century, pioneers set out in earnest for a new life in the Western United States, and the scattering of families became an American tradition, reaching its apex during the Great Depression of the 1930s. Continuing into the present, as corporations transfer employees to wherever they are needed, it is more for economic reasons than for adventure that families are sundered, and the extended family, generations living under the same roof, has become nostalgia.

Another type of leaving home is a spiritual one, stemming from a long tradition of sauntering pilgrims and mendicant monks. Leaving home is also a metaphor for leaving the isolated home of one's ego for the collective world of the soul, and arriving at the insight: How different I am from my Self!

> Open the door,
> Walk outside—
> It's raining!
>
> Writing a poem
> Outside, wind
> Ruffles words

35
The Uncanny

DAVID:

Ten days before leaving for Italy (January 27, 2003) to teach at Texas A&M University's *Santa Chiara Study Center* in Castiglion Fiorentino, I went to Tucson, Arizona, to give another lecture and workshop on "The Healing Spirit of Haiku." This experience was a prelude to my upcoming three months in Tuscany and many moments of solitude and peace in Nature.

> Quiet courtyard
> Goldfish in murky pond—
> Tree full of oranges

> Old olive tree
> Next to young palm—
> Dove flies by

Reflecting on standing alone in the inner square, I thought of Suzuki's illuminating words, "Where *satori* flashes there is the tapping of creative energy; where creative energy is felt, art breathes *myo* [mystery] and *yūgen* [cloudy impenetrability]."[94] I could not clearly see the goldfish, symbol of transformation, but the tree of life was full of oranges! The second haiku adds two more trees, rooted in Mother Earth and representative of hope for "divine grace." The dove, a universal symbol of peace, allows us a "glimpse into the Unfathomable."[95]

JOEL:

Yūgen is a term used in the philosophy of *Noh* drama for something felt but that can't be expressed. Silent beauty. "Yugen Noh" plays are usually about an encounter with the ghost of a famous person. First a priest on a pilgrimage to some famous place appears, chanting the site's history. Then, wearing a mask, the main character, or *shite,* strangely informed as to subtleties of the history of the place, appears, and a poetic dialogue ensues. Admitting that he, or she, is the ghost of a famous person who lived there, the *shite* asks the priest to pray for him, then vanishes. In the second half of the play, the *shite* reappears in its true form.

Sigmund Freud's *unheimlich* is often translated as "the uncanny,"[96] something indescribable yet strangely familiar, usually terrifying because it violates the categories of explanation. The uncanny bridges the psychic boundaries between life and death, self and other, real and unreal.

> In a basin of clear water,
> I can't see my
> Self

36

Incompleteness

DAVID:

I'd been in Castiglion Fiorentino for five days and it was another gorgeous day. I took a long five-mile walk from the walled Medieval city and went far out into the countryside. I found myself in a valley where Leonardo da Vinci once worked. Although there was a cold north wind, I felt warm inside. I wrote two haiku in celebration of my being blessed with the opportunity to spend part of my life in this special place.

> Bare grapevines stand out
> Under bright Tuscan sun—
> Sole rose bud opens

> Lone white duck
> Beneath naked fruit trees—
> Olive grove, silvery green

JOEL:

Perhaps it is true, as Freud contended,[97] that Leonardo's prodigious creative energy was a sublimation of his homosexuality. If so, there is the irony of his being the model of the Renaissance Man, someone who is gifted and works in several fields at the same time. In Leonardo's case, as he was adept in both art and science, one can speculate that his libido was androgynous. More interesting to me, however, is that he completed few paintings, and much of his scientific work, except for the immediate application of military engineering, never got past the stage of speculative drawings.

All creative endeavors are an exercise in incompleteness, and the art of haiku is no exception. There is always something left out, something grandly referential. Healing, too, is not about being complete, but of being an integrated part of a largely inaccessible world.

> To be poor
> Amidst all these riches—
> Tea kettle whistles

> Across the street,
> Church bells
> Stir my coffee

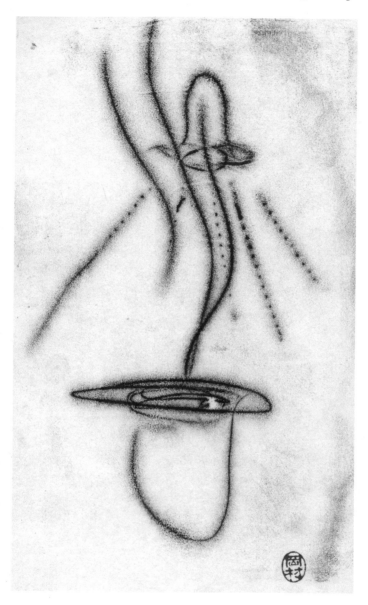

Across the street,

Church bells

Stir my coffee

37
The Feminine Side of the Psyche

DAVID:

As a man, I have been known to project my *anima* (the feminine side of my psyche) onto a woman—particularly if I don't know her. It has happened on airplanes, in dreams (once I made love with a beautiful dark woman with long black hair), and in fantasy (sometimes through women in soap operas, novels, and films, or with women I see but don't know). So on Valentine's Day I wrote:

> Happy Valentine's—
> Water glistening
> Two ducks together

Later I saw a couple walking:

> She grasps with the left
> He grasps with the right—
> Bright February full moon

JOEL:

It's as if my interior life only began when reaching out to the Other. I still remember the blonde girl in grade school who ignored me, leaving me in tears. And the blonde girl in the mountains, where my family spent summers, who refused to return a kiss. She was eleven, a woman; I was a boy of nine.

My first real girlfriend's hair was also blonde, though bleached. Attraction to this hue remained until around age forty, when my longing for light began to turn toward darker realms. I'm talking of inner growth, of course, as a sunny penumbra can still dilate my eyes.

What happened to red?

> Before blossoming,
> Japanese Flowering Cherry Tree
> Is modestly red

38
Rome

DAVID:

After visiting the Coliseum and Vatican in Rome, I had another expe-
rience of *anima* projection following leaving a bar by the fountain of
four turtles:

> Tilted lamp unlit
> Rushing Tiber river—
> Lovers embrace

Walking by the river, I stopped under a tree:

> Overhanging branches
> Sound of water—
> A star appears

JOEL:

The Coliseum and the Roman Catholic Church share the same history, and the Vatican fills its cup of sacrificial blood from those cruelly heroic days when martyrs prayed before the open jaws of their darker selves.

Summer night—
Behind fan's *hum*
A motorcycle roars

39
Italy

David:

Leaving Rome with a free weekend, I ended up on the magical Isle of Capri—a place I'd heard about and seen only in films. It was as lovely as I'd been led to believe. I walked up to Mt. Tiberio where Emperors Augustus and later Tiberius built palaces about two thousand years ago. The view was spectacular. Looking over a cliff a thousand feet high, across emerald waters, I could see all of Capri and even Sorrento and the Amalfi Coast. Coming through arches, I turned and saw:

> Goats stare and chew
> On wall of Imperial Quarters
> At Villa Jovis

The Buddha was right—nothing is permanent: all that remains here are walls with goats on them—and they too will disappear.

Joel:

The Italian master storyteller, Italo Calvino, relates how Marco Polo told Kublai Khan about the streets of Cecilia, where "I met once a goatherd, driving a tinkling flock along the walls, who asked him what city they were in."[98] Marco was amazed by the question, as the spectacular city was easily recognizable. The goatherd explained that he was unable to tell one city from another, although he knew by name all the grazing lands between them. On the other hand, Marco only knew built places, while uninhabited space, their rocks and trees, all looked the same to him.

> Late afternoon—
> A street sign's shadow
> Points the way

Years later, Marco was lost in a city, and who did he meet but the same goatherd. Marco asked what city they were in. The old man replied, "Cecilia, worse luck!" Marco cried that this was impossible. He had entered a city far from Cecilia, and had kept going deeper into it. How could this be Cecilia? "The places have mingled," the goatherd said. "Cecilia is everywhere."[99]

> Bubbles rising
> On the waterfall
> Are water too

40

St. Francis of Assisi

DAVID:

I love Assisi! How appropriate to be in this sacred place as the United States prepared for war with Iraq. I walked to the *Santuario Eremo delle Carceri,* a hermitage in the mountains several miles above the city. It is a solitary place where one can be alone and pray. This is where St. Francis would retreat to his cell and pray, and in the surrounding woods bless Mother Earth and her animals. The sound of birds and the Spirit of St. Francis were everywhere. Later, walking down the mountain in the twilight, I composed these haiku:

> At Assisi
> Silent olive branches—
> Pray for peace

> Olive leaves glitter
> As sun sets
> Over Assisi

JOEL:

When St. Francis was a child, he ran away from home to be an oblate, taking with him some family money, which he gave to a priest.[100] When he returned home, his father beat him, and locked him in the cellar, threatening further punishment if he persisted on that path. He wanted his son to be a businessman like him. Because of this, St. Francis failed to identify with his father, bonding with his sympathetic mother.

As an adult, he assumed the role of a mother to the men of his Order. If he had been close to his father, if his animus had been in ascension, would his relationship to the earth have been more from the dictates of God the Father, of ownership, not stewardship, of domination instead of interdependency? We do know that St. Francis was an androgynous figure: a man in flesh, a woman in spirit, which is what made his spiritual life so radical, and difficult to exemplify.

> Bite into
> An olive,
> To the pit

41
Looks Like Big Sur

DAVID:

Over their Spring break, two of my daughters, Laura and Rachel, visited me in Italy. I met them in Rome and we went to Santa Chiara in Castiglion Fiorentino, where we stayed for a few days. We then went on a field trip with other students and professors to Ravenna (the Byzantine mosaics are worth the trip) and Venice (with its unique canals, churches, and culture). In Padua we saw Giotto's frescoes and tasted the best gelato! We then took a train to Verona and experienced this enchanting city.

The next day, my daughters returned to America and I headed for the isle of Corfu. I stayed with a dear friend, Anthony Stevens, who had moved there recently from England. I had never visited this unusually green Greek island. However, I had always wanted to go there, since reading about it in books by Lawrence Durrell. Anthony was a gracious host and each day we set out from his "Corfiot Villa" in Vassilika for a different part of the island. One day we went from the main port city of Kerkyra north to Mount Pantokrator. It was a long curvy ride and at midday we stopped in the village of Strinilas at a family taverna. At the top, where you could see snow-capped mountains in Albania, sat a monastery dating from the tenth century, with a huge antenna straddling its old courtyard and walls. It was a strange mixture of ancient spirituality and modern technology.

Another day we drove north, on the western side of the island up a mountainous road. The views were even more breathtaking than the day before. High above Paleokastritsa, a beautiful bay and resort area, the coast looked like the Big Sur area in Northern California. The whole island was verdant and covered with trees: olive, umbrella and stone pine, juniper, cedar, and white oak. Vineyards filled the valleys.

On the northwest shoreline is Cape Drastis.

> Walk through olive groves
> A peaceful silence—
> Wild flowers everywhere

> Sun on sea
> Swaying bamboo—
> Bay of sculpted cliffs

JOEL:

A Chinese man was being driven from Santa Fe to Taos. As the automobile reached the plateau on which the town is located, a spectacular sight, he exclaimed, "This looks like China! This looks like home!" Just so, the Oregon Coast looks like Big Sur, California, especially on stormy days.

> Churning waters—
> Rocks look like
> Poseidon's eyebrows

42
Two Chapels

DAVID:

On a Sunday in late March at Santa Chiara, I was sitting outside on my balcony in the glorious sun. It was quiet and I was taking it all in:

> Mating butterflies dance
> In olive grove—
> Nesting pigeons coo

Later I took one of my daily meditative walks along a lovely country road out to the *Santuario della Madonna del Bagno,* a church built on the site where a shepherdess saw the Virgin Mary and a spring of water started flowing, which has never stopped!

> Above the stones
> Two wild poppies bloom—
> Vineyard still barren

> Rosemary covers walls
> Bees surround its violet flowers—
> Rooster crows

JOEL:

The chapel I remember most fondly is the *Capilla de Nuestra Señora de Guadeloupe.* Located in the Old Town section of Albuquerque, New Mexico, it was designed by Sister Giotto Muntz, in 1975, as a classroom for Christian iconography. Behind its thick adobe walls, even in the middle of summer a cool darkness prevails, set off to the left by a large round picture window, a mandala that filters, except for candles, the chapel's only source of light. Straight ahead is a shrine for loved ones who have passed away: photos and flowers, votive candles cast shadows day and night. Against opposing walls in the next room, high-backed wooden seats face each other, carved with potent phrases, such as: "The Zeal For Your House Has Eaten Me Up."

Outside are benches, and a garden. Built at the end of an alley, with not too many tourists walking that way, it is usually a peaceful place to sit, ruminate, and write.

One afternoon, emerging from a reverie in the chapel, I found it had rained.

> Summer rain—
> Wildflowers, slowly
> Stand straight again
>
> On the bench—
> Ant runs, rain-
> Drops fall

43
Temenos

DAVID:

In the classroom where I taught two courses, Psychology of Religion and Psychology of Self, I always wrote *temenos*[101] on the board. A pigeon had built a nest on the ledge between the window and a partially open shutter.

> Nesting bird by window
> Egg appears, Easter nears—
> Study of the soul

Joel:

"There was in Athens a sacred precinct (a *temenos*) dedicated to Gaia and surnamed Olympia."[102] A temple built for a god, the *templum* is that portion the Roman augur marked out with his staff as he watched the stars journey across the sky, or perhaps a flight of birds. This evolved into the place where watching was done, an inner sanctuary, a place of observance where only a priest, or priestess, was allowed to enter.

Reverie is one state in which we may enter the soul. Here one becomes an acolyte, able to approach the place that is no-place, the *temenos* of enlightenment, where we may dream the god awake.

Easter Sunday

Wake up!
The creek
Is singing

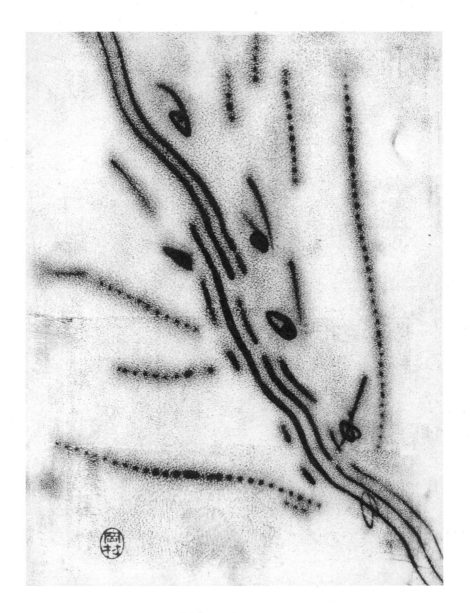

Wake up!
The creek
Is singing

44

Strada a Mammi

DAVID:

In early April 2003, I walked up *Strada a Mammi*. This means "the street to Mammi," which used to be the name of a village and castle—now in ruins—high above Castiglion Fiorentino. It was a magnificent clear day with blue sky, no clouds, lots of sun, and a breeze—at times even a brisk cool wind. Once at the top, I found a meadow in which I lay down and rested.

> Rocky hillside
> Beneath twisted olive tree—
> Poppies blow in the wind

> Fruit saplings blossom
> Before sea of olive trees—
> Red tile roofs beyond

> Lying next to this
> Tiny red wildflower—
> We are of one world

JOEL:

The boy may have slept in this very meadow, dreaming of an heroic future. The village below, into which he was born, although outwardly peaceful, was plagued with gangsters, among whom he had already made some influential friends.

When the Fascists marched in, he joined the Resistance, living in the wilderness, fighting the tyranny that had swallowed his country.

Years later, now a renowned Cardinal, a Prince of the Church, he made a trip home to visit family and old friends. Climbing Strada a Mammi, lying in the meadow of his boyhood again, he was finally able to make peace with himself.

The most healing places are those that reside in niches of memory that harbor images of youthful happiness, even if they are painted in nostalgia's transparent colors. There, from a time of life when anything seemed possible, the whole of creation speaks to us again.

> On the hedge—
> Red flowers bloom,
> Blue, and yellow too
>
> Flowering bushes—
> Weighed with beauty,
> Of which they are aware?

45
Tuscany

DAVID:

One day at the highest point in Castiglion Fiorentino by the Medieval Cassero or tower, I wrote a haiku celebrating spring.

> Under umbrella pines
> Ancient Tuscan Valley—
> Sound of birds

Later I walked out via Madonna del Bagno:

> Church of the Madonna
> Hungry cats swarming around—
> Gentle spring rain

Joel:

Curzio Malaparte wrote that Tuscans "have the gift of seeing people and things not only as they are but as they seem to be."[103] That is, they can see through a person's pretensions, cutting them down to size "with that little Tuscan laugh so meager and green."[104]

Many years ago, English artist John Kielty Bell and I were motorcycling through mountain villages northwest of Tokyo, two tall rough 'n ready Westerners outfitted with black leather jackets riding through the autumn rain. Hungry, we stopped at a vegetable market, striding in like Hell's Angels. Several women looked at us, at each other, then giggled in that shy, polite way Japanese women have.

> Bashō's cultured poems
> Don't have redwoods'
> Rough bark

46
Setting Birds Free

DAVID:

During April we took a field trip to Vinci (near Florence) where Leonardo was born. After the museum in the village, we visited his house in the countryside. He grew up in and around Nature.

> Small miracle—
> Leonardo da Vinci
> Set caged birds free[105]

JOEL:

Po Chu-I (772–846), the great Chinese poet, would buy chickens on their way to market and set them free as a gesture of Buddhist charity. "Limp combs exhausted, in baskets / starved, thirsty, these dammed-up rivers / of sunbeams soaring over Buddha's Garden."[106]

Setting free is an act of compassion. But from what we know of Leonardo, his reasons for setting birds free were more scientific than spiritual. He wanted to observe how they take off and fly in order to build a flying machine and "fill the universe with astonishment."[107]

> Humid morning—
> A mosquito lands
> For breakfast

Small miracle—
Leonardo da Vinci
Set caged birds free

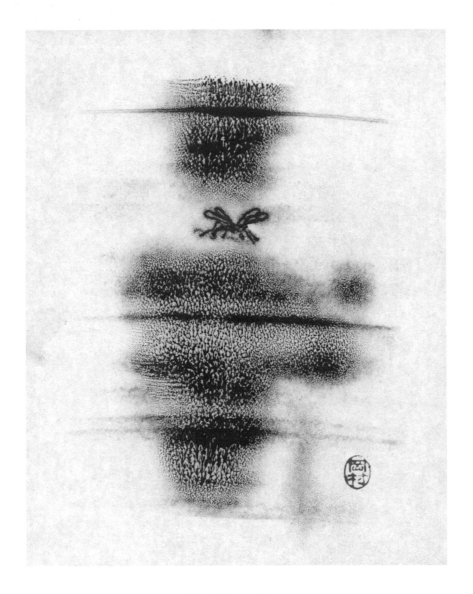

Humid morning—
A mosquito lands
For breakfast

47
Homage to St. Francis

DAVID:

After arriving in Cortona, a pilgrimage: I walked nearly one hour to the remote, almost Asian-like Monastery *Eremo Francescano delle Celle*. It was built in the thirteenth century and has a cell where St. Francis stayed and prayed.

> Moved caterpillars off road
> To wet earth—
> Homage to St. Francis
>
> Dripping wild bamboo—
> Waterfall behind
> Rushing to stones below
>
> Water under bridge
> Moist weeping willow—
> Tibet in Tuscany
>
> Hail storm
> On olive trees—
> Memories of St. Francis

JOEL:

In his poem, "St. Francis and the Sow," Galway Kinnell writes that "everything flowers, / from within, of self-blessing; / though sometimes it is necessary / to reteach a thing its loveliness..."[108]

As we age, our bodies evolve into a form we would rather they not be, so that every day we must learn to accept their contours anew. Some people turn to plastic surgery, in an effort to keep their youthful mask intact. This is okay, as it raises self-esteem. Others turn to flowering from within, which is even better, as it lets the illusion of sustainability to fall.

Kinnell's sow is not old, in fact she is pregnant. However, sows, companions of Demeter, goddess of natural cycles, have naturally creased foreheads. And as St. Francis rested his hand on the sow's forehead, blessing her, "the sow / began remembering all the way down her thick length. . . . to the spiritual curl of her tail..."[109]

> Halo of baldness,
> Round belly—
> Life's circular tale
>
> In the garden—
> A man turns top soil
> Over

48
Two More Weeks

DAVID:

Early one Saturday morning, I opened the shutters and doors to the balcony off my room. Only two more weeks at Santa Chiara.

> Round thunder of spring
> Under Tuscan rain—
> No birds in flight

> Cool April rain
> Wet green fields—
> Smell of the Earth

JOEL:

Only two more weeks! That's what I would say every time I stepped out of the airport and Ft. Lauderdale's heat and humidity hit my face like a hot pie. From the time I went there to say goodbye to my father, who was dying from Alzheimer's Disease, until Mother's funeral eight years later, every year I counted the days until I could return home.

Mother once told me that when I was a child, while she was busy shopping I'd wander off. In those days, at least in that neighborhood, children were comparatively safe. She said that she'd always find me sitting in a doorway.

Man sleeps in doorway—
A pigeon turns its head
This way and that

In 1964, I left my childhood home in Brooklyn, New York, moving to the San Francisco Bay Area, where I began my journey toward what maturity might be. During the vulnerable years of childhood there is unavoidable conditioning that, psychologically, can never be completely overcome. Still, one takes steps toward maturity. We don't grow up, we grow out, we outgrow each step. What's most important is that these steps be decisive.

Growing on the fence,
This grape vine
Doesn't bear fruit

49
Looking and Listening

DAVID:

The next day, it was sunny and warm. I love a walk after rain. I took a longer circular route, walking to *Santuario della Madonna del Bagno*. However, I kept going through more countryside, and looped around to the stadium, returning the back way to Santa Chiara.

> Red poppies
> Lush artichokes—
> Lizard leaps for fly

> Church bells ring
> Dog barks
> Sun shines

> Weeds surround
> Olive tree
> Their flowers bright yellow

> Spring wind
> Scent of blooming rosemary
>   and chicken dung—
> Cuckoo calls

JOEL:

I have known David Rosen more than thirty years, and all that time, comfortable in the world, he has loved to travel, unmasking truths in himself and others.

I have done some traveling, too, but have usually preferred opening to what's at hand. Yet, it has only been a few years since I found a place with the eerie sense of belonging, with an ecosystem that spans

seashore

> Seagull's shadow
> Sweeps over sand,
> My notebook too

mountains

> Walking the trail,
> Stop and listen:
> *Tweet-tweet, tweet-tweet...*

urban center

> On the Bus—
> Chin against book,
> An old man drools words

Seagull's shadow
Sweeps over sand,
My notebook too

50
Field of Elves

DAVID:

For Easter I went to Switzerland to visit my friend Armin (Minu) Schmidt[110] and his wife, Katrin, and their lovely children, Tom and Lisa. They live outside of Bern in a village called Münchenbuchsee. After dinner, Minu and I walked:

> Walking at night
> Through an unfinished golf course—
> Full moon rises

The next day Minu took me to a nature preserve by the Aare river, which was also known as a "field of elves."

> Bridge over brook
> Stones on bottom—
> Birds chirp

JOEL:

Elves, or fairies, are usually regarded as "either non-human nature spirits or else as spirits of the dead."[111] In a few cases they are regarded as "the souls of prehistoric races."[112] After thousands of years, these old beliefs hang on, resisting symbiotic normalization by mainstream religions.

> Which tree
> Falls next?—
> Moss clings to rocks

Instead, they adapt, staring out from the architecture of Gothic cathedrals, hidden in the dark naves of churches, sleeping under dusty synagogue benches, weaving themselves into the abstractions of Islamic filigree, baring the underworld, as turbulent as ever, in Tibetan tankas, in the heat of creativity, in this unfinished, cobbled-together world.

> Climbing the path
> In thin-soled shoes,
> Stones poke through

51
Carving Stone

DAVID:

While at Santa Chiara, I was a student in Alberto Bruni's stone sculpting class. My goal was to carve a *mandala* (magic circle) in stone. Each week when I neared Bruni's workshop, I could hear the tapping from all the hammers hitting chisels cutting stone.

> Sound of stone carving
> Mandala emerges—
> Wisteria blooms

> Maestro Bruni
> Sculpting in stone—
> Healing the soul

JOEL:

Beniamino Benvenuto Bufano was born in San-Fele, Italy, in 1898.[113] His family emigrated to New York City, where he trained as a sculptor at The Art Students League. After traveling for four years around the world, he made a permanent home in San Francisco.

A life-long pacifist, to protest the United States entering World War I, Benny, as he was affectionately known around town, cut off a finger and sent it to President Woodrow Wilson.

But it was his many statues of St. Francis that made him famous. Most were carved from granite and steel, although one he cast entirely from the metal of melted-down guns.

> Finger cut off
> Stands again—
> Body count in Iraq

52
Kindle the Fire

David:

I returned to the United States and my home in Texas in late April to host the Fay Lecture Series in Analytical Psychology at Texas A&M University,[114] delivered by Stanton Marlan, May 2–4, 2003. His topic, "The Black Sun: The Alchemy and Art of Darkness," involved the creative, spiritual, and healing aspects of depression.

A week later, I was out on my deck having coffee and breakfast in the healing sun. There was a warm breeze and birds were singing.

> Wind blows
>
> Sun shines
>
> Birds call—
>
> What else is there?

After a long day's work and my daily meditative walk, it was dusk. I made myself comfortable on a bench built into my deck.

> Sitting down by the jasmine
>
> Fragrance of late spring—
>
> Fireflies appear

JOEL:

Jewish Cabbalists believe that there is a Torah that predates the creation of this universe. It is called the Unfolded Torah, or the Torah of Grace. The *Midrash Konen* tells us that this pre-existent Torah, which is not the one rolled open in synagogues, was written "in black fire on white fire."[115]

One flame brands the other: the black, or esoteric, marks the white, or literal. "Endless consuming of sacred parchment and profane page given over to signs,"[116] wrote French/Jewish poet Edmond Jabès, commenting on this mystery.

We can read the Testaments, Old and New, the Koran, the Sutras, we can read to the end of our days.

> In the vase,
> Artificial flowers
> Seem real

53
Turtle Wisdom

DAVID:

I love turtles. In Native American teachings, turtles are symbolic of Mother Earth or Nature. My psyche and home are filled with turtles and slow going is the only Way for me. The old fable of the tortoise and the hare is my story! When you embrace the turtle symbol, "You are being asked to honor the creative source within you, to be grounded to the Earth, and to observe your situation with motherly compassion. . . . Turtle buries its thoughts, like its eggs, in the sand, and allows the sun to hatch the little ones. This teaches you to develop your ideas before bringing them out in the light."[117]

> *Kame* calls
> Listen to the ancient
> Voice of Mother Earth[118]

Joel:

The Shang Oracle of China, recently unearthed, used turtle shells to divine everything from the weather to success in hunting and war.[119] The shell would be heated until cracks appeared, the shapes of which would be interpreted. The turtle was also honored for its longevity, which was said to have to do with its slow breathing. It has been compared to a mendicant sage, for carrying its shelter with it, and the wisdom of its pace.

Legend has it that one day the English physicist Sir Arthur Eddington was giving a lecture on cosmological mythologies, one of which is the Indian belief that the universe rests on the back of a giant turtle. However, Eddington opined, if this is true, on what does the turtle stand?

After the lecture, Eddington was approached by an elderly woman who told him that he didn't understand Indian cosmology. "You are very clever, young man, very clever, but it's turtles all the way down."[120]

> Older than I thought I'd ever be—
> Across the path,
> Acorns are scattered

Postscript

Unless the soul goes out to meet what we see, we do not see it;
nothing do we see, not a beetle, not a blade of grass.
—W.H. HUDSON[121]

JOEL:

David, when we began to work on this book, we had no precon-
ceptions. We didn't have a format, not even a title, only an idea of
exchanging poems on healing and the practice of haiku. It became a
journey, the kind of which I had not imagined. What amazes me is
that although each of our lives unfolded very differently, we found
that we share certain landscapes and philosophies.

Midsummer heat—

Seeds sprout

Inside and out

David:

Joel, we've clearly been on a journey to the Soul and our souls have touched one another. Our healing haibuns are very personal yet universal. My hunch is that what we've written will stir others and they'll react in unplanned ways and begin pilgrimages into Nature in the spirit of *Eros*. The haiku that follows was composed after being with a woman friend.

> Soft touch of your fingers
> On my worn face—
> Gentle mist[122]

The next poem was written standing on the beach by the sea: The ultimate source.

> Wave upon wave upon wave
> Sifting sand sifting sand—
> New shells appear

Henry Wadsworth Longfellow echoes the same sentiment:

> *Nothing that is shall perish utterly,*
> *But perish only to revive again.*
> *In other forms. . .* [123]

Notes

1. Auden, W.H. "The Art of Healing." In *Collected Poems,* edited by Edward Mendelson, 626–628. New York: Random House, 1976.
2. Blyth, R.H. *A History of Haiku, Vol. 1.* Tokyo: Hokuseido Press, 1963, p. 28.
3. Nye, Naomi Shihab. This quote is from "The Poetry of Listening," the Sixth Annual Harry A. Wilmer III Memorial Lecture. The Institute of the Humanities, Salado, TX, June 1, 2003.
4. According to Arthur Okamura, his monoprints "are made by rolling black oil paint on a sheet of glass, very smoothly, paper is placed on top and impressions are made from the back of the paper through drawing with pencils, combs, fingers, etc."
5. Haiku can also be in a non-traditional form with a varied number of syllables less than 17.
6. Matsuo Kinsaku (1644–1694) was born in a town near Kyoto. A young poet with a growing reputation, he was given a cottage, named *Bashō An,* "Banana Tree Hermitage." Henceforth he would be known as Bashō.
7. Blyth, R.H. *A History of Haiku, Vol. 1 & 2.* Tokyo: Hokuseido Press, 1963, 1964. Suzuki, Daisetz. "Zen and Haiku." In *Zen and Japanese Culture,* edited by Daisetz Suzuki, 217–267. New York: Pantheon, 1959.
8. *Senryu* is a form of haiku, primarily concerned with human nature and often humorous.
9. Rosen, D.H. "Inborn basis for the doctor-patient relationship." *The Pharos* 55 (1992): 17–21.
10. Nagayama, Aya. *Susuki-To-Ya.* Tokyo: Asahi Newspaper Company, 2001.

11. Rosen, D.H. *The Tao of Jung: The Way of Integrity.* New York: Penguin, 1997.

12. Chodorow, Joan, ed. *Jung on Active Imagination.* Princeton, NJ: Princeton University Press, 1997.

13. A *haibun*, which combines prose and haiku, is about a journey.

14. A *haigu* is a drawing or illustration with a haiku.

15. Shirane, Haruo. *Traces of Dreams: Landscape, Cultural Memory and the Poetry of Bashō.* Stanford, CA: Stanford University Press, 1998, p. 227.

16. *Ibid.,* p.161.

17. *Ibid.,* p. 81.

18. *Ibid.,* p. 115.

19. Blyth, R. H., op. cit., in note 7.

20. Higginson, William. *The Haiku Handbook.* New York: McGraw-Hill, 1985.

21. Alone is derived from "all One."

22. Shirane, Haruo, op. cit., p. 45 in note 15.

23. When I was an eighteen-year-old exchange student in Greece, my Greek brother, Alex Tritsibidas, shared this philosophy with me. Now I know it is true and the haiku moment, as well as the creative response, expresses it extremely well.

24. Achterberg, Jeanne. *Imagery and Healing: Shamanism and Modern Medicine.* Boston: Shambhala, 1985, p. 17.

25. Rosen, D.H. *Transforming Depression: Healing the Soul Through Creativity, 3rd ed.* York Beach, ME: Nicolas-Hays, 2002, p. xxi.

26. Oman, Maggie, ed. *Prayers for Healing.* Berkeley, CA: Conari Press, 1997, p. 265.

27. I have no record of the first haiku I wrote as a child at McDaniel Elementary School in Springfield, Missouri. However, I know from what has transpired that a seed was planted deep in my psyche.

28. Rosen, D.H. op. cit., in note 25.

29. Rosen, D.H. *Modern Haiku* xxix(1)(1998): Winter-Spring, p. 27.

30. Lao Tzu, *Tao Te Ching,* trans. S. Mitchell. New York: Harper Collins, 1988, No. 1.

31. Rosen, D.H., op. cit., in note 11.

32. Rosen, D.H. *Psychological Perspectives* 47 (2004).

33. Thoreau, Henry David. *Walking: A Little Book of Wisdom.* San Francisco: HarperSanFrancisco, 1994, pp. 1, 2, 5, 6.

34. Rosen, D.H. op cit., in note 29.

35. *Ibid.*

36. *Ibid.*

37. *Ibid.*

38. Chang, Chung-yuan. *Tao: A New Way of Thinking.* New York: Harper & Row, 1977, p. 84.

39. *Ibid.*

40. Oman, Maggie. op. cit., P. 214, in note 26.

41. Rosen, D.H. op cit., in note 29.

42. Goodman, Felicitas. *Where the Spirits Ride the Wind.* Bloomington, IN: Indiana University Press, 1990.

43. Bashō, Matsuo. *The Narrow Road to the Deep North and Other Travel Sketches,* translated by N. Yuasa. Baltimore, MD: Penguin, 1966, pp. 72 & 156.

44. These 1995 Fay Lectures evolved into a book: Kawai, Hayao. *Buddhism and the Art of Psychotherapy,* College Station, TX: Texas A&M University Press, 1996.

45. My father was a physician in the Navy during World War II and assigned to a battalion of marines fighting the Japanese in the South Pacific. When I was born on February 25, 1945, the Red Cross attempted to notify my father, but my mother was told he was "Missing in Action." He was sent home shell-shocked after his amphibious landing craft was blown up by the Japanese during an invasion of one of the islands. His soul and mine were troubled as far back as I can remember.

46. *Koi* is the Japanese word for carp.

47. Letter to Countess Solms-Laubach, 3 August 1907. Quoted in "The Essential Solitude." In *The Siren's Song: Selected Essays of Maurice Blanchot,* edited by Gabriel Josipovici. Bloomington, IN: Indiana University Press, 1982, p. 97.

48. I call this "egocide" and it is defined and described in Rosen, D.H. op. cit., pp. xxi & xxiv, in note 25. In this case, it was the part of my ego connected to a painful relationship with my father.

49. Shigematsu, Sōiku, ed. & trans. *Zen Haiku: Poems and Letters of Natsume Sōseki.* New York: Inklings/Weatherhill, 1994, pp. 12 & 13.

50. Rosen, D.H. op. cit., in note 32.

51. Oman, Maggie. op. cit., p. 80, in note 26.

52. Kawai, Hayao. op. cit., p. 21, in note 44.

53. Rosen, D.H. op. cit., in note 32.

54. Lao Tzu. *Hua Hu Ching (The Unknown Teachings of Lao Tzu),* translated by B. Walker. San Francisco: HarperSanFrancisco, 1992, p. 98.

55. Weston, Anthony. *Back to Earth: Tomorrow's Environmentalism.* Philadelphia: Temple University Press, 1994, p. 58.

56. Rosen, D.H. *Modern Haiku* xxxi(1)(2000): Winter-Spring, p. 8.

57. Mountain, Marian. *The Zen Environment.* New York: Bantam Books, 1983, p. 33.

58. Rosen, D.H. *Modern Haiku* xxxi(2)(2000): Summer, p. 4.

59. Shimano, Eido. Endless Vow: *The Zen Path of Soen Nakagawa,* translated by K. Tanahashi & R. S. Chayat. Boston & London: Shambhala, 1996, p. 122.

60. Rosen, D.H. op. cit., in note 32.

61. Weishaus, J. "The Deeds and Sufferings of Light." See: http://www.cddc.vt.edu/host/weishaus/cont-r.htm.

62. Green rocks are made of trinitite, a greenish glassy substance that was formed from sand in the extreme heat of the atomic blast at Ground Zero. "At one time Trinitite completely covered the depression made by the (nuclear) explosion. Afterwards the depression was filled and much of the Trinitite was taken away..." (from the Trinity Site — A National Historic Landmark. White Sands Missile Range, NM, Public Affairs Office).

63. Rosen, D.H. *Modern Haiku* xxxiii(2)(2002): Summer, p. 39.

64. Rosen, D.H. In *Intersections. Members' Anthology,* edited by A.C. Missias. New York: Haiku Society of America, 1999, p. 31.

65. *Rytaku-ji,* "Temple of the Pond Dragon," is located above Mishima City, about halfway between Tokyo and Kyoto. The Abbot at the time was Nakagawa Soen, Roshi.

66. Bashō, M. op. cit., in note 43.

67. *Ibid.,* p. 28.

68. *Sugi* trees are tall, sturdy, and ancient. They are related to Redwood trees.

69. Rosen, D.H. In *Haiku Society of America Members' Anthology,* 2002, edited by J. Ball, Naia, & W. Wright. Winchester, VA: Red Moon Press, 2003, p. 56.

70. Rosen, D.H. op. cit., in note 32.

71. Rosen, D.H. In *Crinkled Sunshine,* edited by D.C. Gallagher. Members' Anthology. New York: Haiku Society of America, 2000, p. 41.

72. Jay Stattman, one of the first therapists to use the T-group technique, moved to Europe where he founded his own school of healing. At age fifty-three, Dr. Stattman died in Amsterdam from a massive heart attack on the day his wife, a Dutch physician, was going to tell him she was pregnant with their third child.

73. Kawai, Hayao. *Dreams, Myths & Fairy Tales in Japan.* Einsiedeln, Switzerland: Daimon, 1995, p. 13.

74. *Hototogisu* is the Japanese word for the cuckoo.

75. "... Coleridge asked..." "What if you slept, and what if in your sleep you dreamed, and what if in your dreams you went to heaven and there you plucked a strange and beautiful flower, and what if when you awoke you had the flower in your hand? Ah, what then?" Samuel Taylor Coleridge.

    The thought/image was first expressed by STC in a notebook entry in 1815 or 1816. See: *Anima Poetae: From the Unpublished Notebooks of Samuel Taylor Coleridge,* edited by E. Hartley Coleridge. London: W. Heinemann, 1895.

    "The notebook entry reads: "If a man could pass thro' Paradise in a Dream, & have a flower presented to/ him as a pledge that his Soul had really been there, / & found that flower in his hand when he awoke—/ Aye! And what then?" —Petra Backonja in an email to Joel Weishaus, June 17, 2003.

76. *Ikebana* is the word for floral arrangement in Japanese.

77. Onitsura cited in D.H. Rosen's foreword to Hayao Kawai's *Buddhism and the Art of Psychotherapy.* op. cit., p. XII, in note 44.

78. "Apes were to become men, in the incredible wisdom of nature, because flowers had produced seeds and fruits in such tremendous quantities that a new and totally different store of energy had become available in concentrated form." Eiseley, Loren. *How Flowers Changed the World.* San Francisco: Sierra Club, 1996.

79. The Rothko Chapel was financed by the Ménil Foundation, and is located on the campus of The University of St. Thomas, Houston, Texas. The paintings were made between 1964 and 1967. Rothko committed suicide in 1970, a year before the chapel was built.

80. "The problem of the searing Texas light could not be solved and it was only at certain moments late in the day that the chapel took on a semblance of the sacred aura so many have felt in Rothko's studio." Ashton, Dore. *About Rothko.* New York: Oxford University Press, 1983, p. 184.

81. To understand this, one must know: My sister and brother-in-law met when she was fourteen and he was sixteen. They married four years later. Thus, at the time of Mother's funeral, my brother-in-law had been a part of the family for more than fifty years. He also told me that he and my father had achieved a close relationship, something I hadn't known.

82. *Susuki* is the Japanese word for Pampas grass.

83. Berger, John. *Photocopies.* New York: Pantheon Books, 1996, p. 53.

84. See: *Japanese Death Poems: Written by Zen Monks and Haiku Poets on the Verge of Death,* compiled with an Introduction by Yoel Hoffman. Rutland, VT: Charles E. Tuttle, 1986.

85. Hillman, James. *Anima: An Anatomy of a Personified Notion.* Dallas, TX: Spring Publications, 1985, p. 143.

86. Weishaus, J. "This Side of the World: Selected Poems."
    See: http://www.cddc.vt.edu/host/weishaus/cont-p.htm.

87. Bach, Richard. *Illusions: The Adventures of a Reluctant Messiah.*
    New York: Delcorte Press, 1977, p. 134.

88. Jung, C.G. *The Archetypes and the Collective Unconscious.*
    Collected Works. Princeton, NJ: Princeton University Press, 1977,
    p. 26.

89. Rosen, D.H. *The Tao of Elvis.* San Diego: Harcourt, 2002.

90. Thoreau, Henry David. op. cit., p. 16, in note 33.

91. Rosen, D.H. op. cit., in note 32.

92. Merton, Thomas, and Nestor, Sarah. *Woods, Shore,*
    Desert: A Notebook, May 1968. Foreword by Brother Patrick
    Hart. Introduction and Notes by Joel Weishaus Santa Fe, NM:
    Museum of New Mexico Press, 1982.

93. Patrick de Sercey is the author of *Being Space.* Santa Fe,
    NM: Moon Bear Press, 1991, which psychologist John White
    called "a startling blend of Existential, Buddhist and Jungian
    thought."

94. Suzuki, Daisetz, op. cit., pp. 220 & 221, in note 7.

95. *Ibid.*

96. See: "The Uncanny." In *The Standard Edition of the*
    Complete Psychological Works of Sigmund Freud, Vol. xvii.
    Edited by James Strachey. London: Hogarth, 1953, pp. 219–252.

97. Freud, Sigmund. *Leonardo da Vinci and a Memory of His*
    Childhood. New York: Norton, 1964.

98. Calvino, Italo. *Invisible Cities,* translated by W. Weaver. New
    York: Harcourt Brace Jovanovich, 1972, pp. 153–153.

99. *Ibid.*

100. Gelber, Hester Goodenough. "A Theater of Virtue: The
     Exemplary World of St. Francis of Assisi." In *Saints and*

Virtues, edited by John Stratton Hawley. Berkeley, CA: University of California Press, 1987, pp. 15–35.

101. *Temenos* is Greek and means "a sacred space."

102. Jung, C.G. *Symbols of Transformation: The Collected Works of C.G. Jung, Vol* 5., translated by R.F.C. Hull. Princeton, NJ: Princeton University Press, 1956, p. 364.

103. Malaparte, Curzio. *Those Cursed Tuscans.* Athens: Ohio University Press, 1963, pp. 114–115.

104. *Ibid.*

105. MacCurdy, Edward, ed. *The Notebooks of Leonardo da Vinci.* New York: George Braziller, 1958, p. 61. "Vasari states Leonardo was in the habit of paying the price demanded by the owners of captive birds simply for the pleasure of setting them free."

106. From "Five Spring Poems From Po Chu-I." See: http://www.cddc.vt.edu/host/weishaus/Poetry/five.htm.

107. Nilson, Peter. "Winged Man and Flying Ships: Of Medieval Flying Journeys and Eternal Dreams of Flight." *Georgia Review* L(2)(1996): Summer, pp. 267–296.

108. Kinnell, Galway *New and Selected Poems.* Boston: Houghton Mifflin, 2000, p. 98.

109. *Ibid.*

110. I first met Minu, a psychologist and professor, in 1995 when a mutual friend arranged for me to stay at his farm house near Bern. I was on a writing retreat, after giving lectures at the Jung Institute in Zurich. He was separated and I was divorced at the time and we became fast and good friends.

111. Evans-Wentz, W.Y. *The Fairy-Faith in Celtic Countries.* New Hyde Park, NY: University Books, 1966, p. 235.

112. *Ibid.*

113. Falk, Randolph. *Bufano.* Millbrae, CA: Celestial Arts, 1975.

114. These annual lectures, endowed by Carolyn Grant Fay, subsequently are published by Texas A&M University Press. David Rosen coordinates these lectures and functions as the General Editor for the Fay Book Series in Analytical Psychology, which in 2004 numbered ten volumes.

115. Scholem, Gershom, "The Oral and the Written." Quoted in Waldrop, Rosmarie, *Lavish Absense: Recalling and Rereading Edmond Jabès.* Middletown, CT: Wesleyan University Press, 2002, p. 110.

116. Jabès, Edmund, "Letter to Jacques Derrida on the Question of the Book." Quoted in Waldrop, Rosmarie, *ibid.,* p. 110.

117. Sams, Jamie, and Carson, David. *Medicine Cards: The Discovery of Power Through the Ways of Animals.* Santa Fe, NM: Bear & Company, 1988, pp. 77 & 78.

118. *Kame* is the Japanese word for turtle.

119. See *People's Daily Online:* April 10, 2003, "China recently unearthed again oracle bones of the Shang Dynasty (C. 16–11TH century B.C.) in Daxinzhuang Shang ruins, more than 100 years later of (sic.) the nation's first discovery of inscribed animal bones and tortoise shells in Anyang City of central China's Henan Province. . . . The inscribed bones found this time are from four 'tanfang' of Shang culture layers. Eight pieces carrying Chinese characters have been sorted out, four of them could be pieced together into a whole page, including 25 characters. They have been confirmed, through the shape of bones, character and grammar, to belong to the same group of inscriptions unearthed in Anyang City a century ago." Li, Heng, "China Unearthed Shang Oracle Bones Again."

120. See: http://www.geocities.com/ilian73/eddington.html. In *A Brief History of Time.* New York: Bantam Books, 1988. Stephen

Hawking tells a similar story, only this time the ubiquitous Turtle Lady lectures the philosopher Bertrand Russell.

121. See: http://myweb.tiscali.co.uk/toddington.poetry/quotes.htm.
122. Rosen, D.H. In D. Lanoue, ed. *Members' Anthology.* New York: Haiku Society of America, 2003, p. 43.
123. Longfellow cited in *Immortality* by Ashley Montagu. New York: Grove Press, 1955, p. 20.

Biographies

The Authors

David Rosen (a physician, psychiatrist, and Jungian psychoanalyst) was born in Portchester, New York, and raised in New York, Texas, Missouri, and California. In 1966, he graduated with a B.A. from the University of California at Berkeley in Psychological-Behavioral Sciences and in 1970 obtained a M.D. from the University of Missouri, Columbia. He did his internship at San Francisco General Hospital and his psychiatric training at the Langley Porter Institute at the University of California at San Francisco (UCSF). Since 1975 he has been in academic medicine and psychiatry at UCSF, the University of Rochester, and at Texas A&M University, where his current primary position is McMillan Professor of Analytical Psychology and his secondary positions are Professor of Humanities in Medicine and Professor of Psychiatry & Behavioral Science. He has written seven other books including *Medicine as a Human Experience* with David Reiser (1985), *The Tao of Jung: The Way of Integrity* (1997), *Transforming Depression: Healing the Soul Through Creativity* (3RD ed. 2002), and *The Tao of Elvis* (2002). He has over a hundred other publications to his credit, including articles, chapters, essays, and haiku poetry. He has a long-standing interest in spirituality and the healing process. He now makes his home in College Station, Texas, is the father of three daughters, and has two grandsons. His webpage is http://psychology. tamu.edu/Faculty/Rosen/index.html.

Joel Weishaus was born in Brooklyn, New York. While still in his teens, he was a Junior Executive for a Madison Avenue advertising

173

agency, a position he left soon after his twenty-first birthday in order to lead the life of a poet, writer, art and literary critic, and visual artist. In 1967–1968, Weishaus was the Literary Editor of the *Daily Californian,* the University of California's student newspaper. He also helped build an experimental theater in San Francisco Haight-Ashbury District. In 1968, he made a trip to Japan, visiting Zen monasteries and fellow poets. In 1971, he edited *On the Mesa: An Anthology of Bolinas Writing,* published by City Lights Books, and *Oxherding: A Reworking of the Zen Text,* with Block Prints by Arthur Okamura. During the next six years, Weishaus did a one-year hermitage in a mountain cabin in Lake County, California, lived for a year in Cambridge, Massachusetts, where he was a resident of the Cambridge Zen Center, and was an Aikido student in San Francisco. In 1977, he moved to New Mexico, where he wrote the Introduction and Notes for Thomas Merton's *Woods, Shore, Desert* (Museum of New Mexico Press, 1983), was an Adjunct Curator at the University of New Mexico's Fine Arts Museum, and a Writer-in-Residence at UNM's Center for Southwest Research. Weishaus presently lives in Portland, Oregon, where he is Visiting Faculty in Portland State University's Department of English (http://web.pdx.edu/~pdx00282).

THE ILLUSTRATOR

ARTHUR OKAMURA was born in Long Beach, California. When he was nine years old, Pearl Harbor was bombed by Japan, and he and his family were interned for nearly three-and-a-half years, the first six months at the Santa Anita (race track) "Assembly Center" and then three years at the Amache Relocation Center, in Colorado. After the war, his family moved to Chicago, Illinois, where he finished public schools. He attended the Art Institute of Chicago, receiving a Ryerson Fellowship, allowing him and his wife to live in Mallorca. There he met the poet Robert Creeley, with whom he became life-long friends, and fellow collaborators on several books. In 1957, Okamura moved to San Francisco, from where he exhibited around the country. In 1959, he made a permanent home in Bolinas, California. His books include texts on *Bashō* and *Issa* with Robert Bly and *Oxherding* with Joel Weishaus. His work has won many prizes and is in over thirty public collections, including the San Francisco Museum of Art, the Whitney Museum, and the Smithsonian Museum. Okamura is a Professor Emeritus at the California College of Arts and Crafts in Oakland, California where he has taught for thirty-one years.